Montcalm at the Battle of Carillon (Ticonderoga) (July 8th, 1758)

LOUIS JOSEPH MARQUIS DE MONTCALM

Montcalm at the Battle of Carillon (Ticonderoga) (July 8th, 1758)
A Principal Engagement of the French & Indian War

Maurice Sautai

LEONAUR

Montcalm at the Battle of Carillon (Ticonderoga) (July 8th, 1758)
A Principal Engagement of the French & Indian War
by Maurice Sautai

First published under the title
Montcalm at the Battle of Carillon (Ticonderoga) (July 8th, 1758)

Leonaur is an imprint of Oakpast Ltd

Copyright in this form © 2011 Oakpast Ltd

ISBN: 978-0-85706-641-1 (hardcover)
ISBN: 978-0-85706-642-8 (softcover)

http://www.leonaur.com

Publisher's Notes

Contents

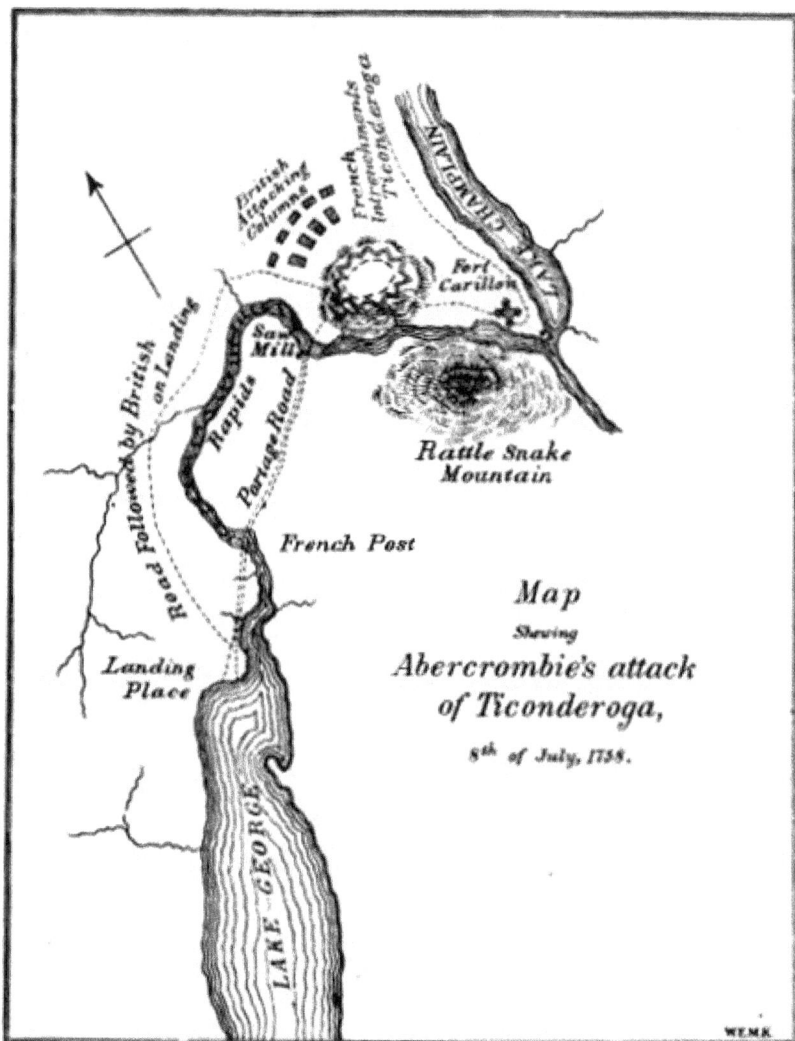

Map

Shewing

Abercrombie's attack
of Ticonderoga,

8th of July, 1758.

CHAPTER 1

Montcalm and His Soldiers

France and Canada, now preparing to offer a supreme appreciation of the Marquis de Montcalm, cannot too highly honour the memory of the heroic General and that of his valiant soldiers, who, following his example, generously shed their blood for the welfare of New France.

The more closely the historian studies the great and noble personality of Montcalm, the deeper he will penetrate into the feelings and the intimate life of his comrades in arms and the more their brilliant qualifications will excite his admiration. Under Montcalm, officers and men of the battalions of the Queen, of Guyenne, of Béarn, of Languedoc, of La Sarre, of Royal-Roussillon and of Berry struggled unflinchingly against a relentless destiny.

Observing them in action at the battle of Carillon, seeing them by their courage alone delaying for a time the course of that fatal destiny, no Frenchman nor Canadian will fail to endorse the opinion of M. de Crémilles, the Lieutenant General charged with the embarkation of our troops for Canada in 1775:

No sovereign in the Universe could have braver or more loyal infantry.

Before beginning the account of the victory of Montcalm at Carillon (Ticonderoga), one should know the condition of affairs in Canada early in 1758 and of the troops entrusted with its defence.

Inspiring England and her colonists with his own virile energy, Pitt wished to endeavour to deliver a final blow to French supremacy in northern America. Whilst he gave to Admiral Boscawen a fleet and a formidable landing force for the reduction of Louisburg, the Dunkirk of our overseas possessions, the Gate of Canada on the Atlantic Ocean, he planned also the invasion of Continental New France. For this purpose, an army of about 16,000 men, comprising in its ranks nearly 10,000 militia and more than 6,000 regulars, under the command of Major General Abercrombie, were to march on Montreal by Lake Champlain and the Richelieu River, capturing on the way the two chief posts of defence of the Colony in that region, Carillon and the fort Saint Frederic, both built on the shore of Lake Champlain. Moreover, Brigadier General John Forbes, with about 7,000 men, of whom nearly 2,000 were regulars, was to drive the French out of the Ohio Valley, after the reduction of Fort Duquesne, their most important post on that river.

To the 23,000 men the English were able to put in line on the Continent, the Governor of Canada, M. de Vaudreuil, could only oppose eight battalions of regulars, making 3,800 men; forty Free companies of marines, numbering a little more than 2,000 men; 3,000 or 4,000 Canadian militia recruits and some savages; altogether about 10,000 men.

The regulars were under the command of Major General the Marquis de Montcalm, who entered the service in 1721 at the age of thirteen, with the rank of ensign in the regiment of Hainaut, of which his father was the Lieutenant Colonel.

Montcalm belonged to a family of Rouergue, concerning whom the glorious tradition ran: "*War is the grave of the Montcalm.*" Wounded in 1746, when colonel of the Auxerrois regiment, at the Battle of Plaisance, he several times rallied his regiment against the charges of the Austrian cavalry and in 1747, at the furious attack on the entrenchments of Assiette, Montcalm won the esteem of the generals under whose command he had fought, amongst others, de Chevert and Marshal de Belle-Isle.

Chosen by d'Argenson early in 1756 to succeed Baron de

Dieskau, commanding the regulars in Canada, wounded and taken prisoner by the English the previous year, Montcalm had proved himself entirely worthy of this appointment by his important success in the capture of Fort Chouaguen (Oswego) in 1756 and of Fort William Henry (or Fort Saint George) in 1757.

As Commander he possessed the qualities which inspire affection: an extreme care for the welfare of the soldier and an equal solicitude for the advancement of his officers, for whom he was never weary of seeking rewards from the King, when they proved themselves worthy.

His plain, very clear instructions and orders are models wherein is revealed a full understanding of the details and a deep knowledge of the military art of his time. Not sparing his own person, brave even to audacity, Montcalm furnished an example for the endurance of fatigue and privations, of the scorn of danger. Intelligence shone in his black eyes, the powder of his wig increasing the effect. *"Ah! How small you are!" cried a savage chieftain meeting him for the first time, "but I see in your eyes the majesty of the oak and the spirit of the eagle."*

The character of Montcalm equalled his military capacity. Firm convictions, an ardent love of France, a high conception of honour, absolute disinterestedness, were its main features. Brought up on Greek and Latin literature, deeply influenced by the reading of Plutarch and Corneille, his soul shared the grandeur of their heroes. In his letters, rapid in style and concise, he reveals himself overflowing with activity, full of fire and subtle irony and interested in intellectual matters. From several points of view Montcalm is associated with the Frenchmen of his century, of that brilliant, so seductive eighteenth century, but he is also and beyond everything a knightly soldier, one of the rare officers of his time, who dared also to take a wide view of affairs.

During the two years Montcalm was in Canada, his honest nature was subjected to a severe test. Before his eyes were exposed each day, with increasing impudence and audacity, the extortions and shameless robberies which undermined the Colony and were to become the principal cause of its loss. Canada was a diseased body of which a corrupt administration was engaged in completing the ruin. An unscrupulous man, of great intelligence, the Lord Lieutenant Bigot, held the finances of the Colony in his all-powerful hands. This grasping man had grouped around himself the persons necessary for his purpose, who had usurped all the commerce of the Colony, foreign and domestic. Under his *aegis* was organized an association, "*La Grande Société*" which seized for itself all branches of exchange, all the offices, all the provisions of food and wood, transportation, public works and treaties with the savages.

If a quarter of the merchandise supposed to have been distributed to them in his name had actually been delivered, the King would have been joined not only by the savages of Canada but also those of all America. No ship entered the St. Lawrence without its cargo being immediately purchased by Bigot and his associates; stored at Quebec in the building the people justly named "*La Friponne*"; exchanged from hand to hand with a growing commission, amongst the members of *La Grande Société* and finally sold to the King, by the last purchaser at a scandalous price.

This pernicious example found imitators in *employés* of all kinds, storage guardians, clerks, who openly adopted the maxim that robbing the King was permissible. As if they had foreseen the approaching ruin of Canada, they hurled themselves on that unhappy Colony in its death throes, harvesting feverishly with absolute impunity the fruit of their plunder.

In the midst of the ruins and of the public misery, Bigot maintained an ostentatious establishment, gambled for such sums as makes one shudder, while the court of his flatterers swarmed about his mistress Madame Péan, the "*Sultana*," distributress of pardons and of favours. She was the wife of a subordinate officer of the Colony, who obligingly closed his eyes to the amours of the Steward and received in compensation an important interest in the manipulation of food stuffs. In a few years he had feloni-

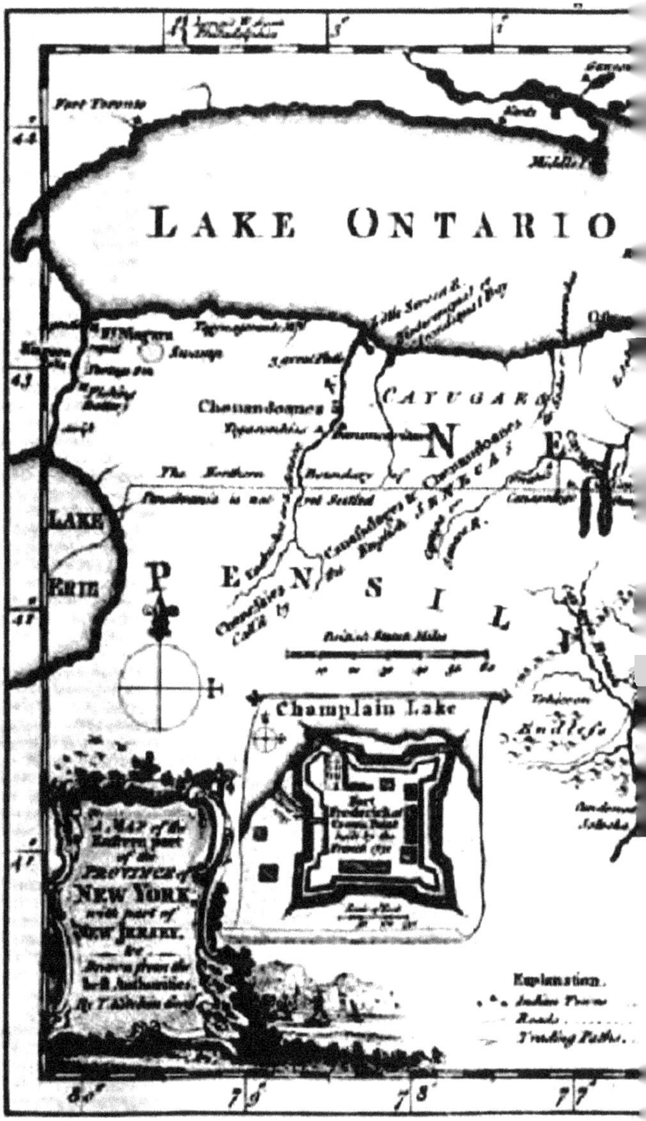
Lake Ontario
Fort Toronto
Champlain Lake
Lake Erie
Chenandoanes
Cayugaes
The Northern Boundary of
Pensilvania is not yet Settled
British Statute Miles
Explanation.
Indian Towns
Roads
Trading Paths.
A MAP of the Eastern part of the PROVINCE of NEW YORK with part of NEW JERSEY, &c. Drawn from the best Authorities. By T. Kitchin

ously accumulated a fortune of several millions.

With Péan, this " *Verrès*" of the Colony, other *protégés* of Bigot entered into rivalry, common people, newly rich, full of insolence and cynicism: Deschenaux, his secretary; Varin, Treasurer of the Navy; Martel, Storage Guardian of Montreal, and the little hunchback Maurin, "a clerk at a low salary, a freak of nature with a face like a snail, travelling with a train of coaches and carryalls, spending more on carriages, on harness, on horses than a young rattle-brained coxcomb of a farmer;" finally Cadet, a butcher transformed to a Commissary General, later convicted of having, with his accomplices, sold to the King, for the sum of twenty-three millions that which had cost him but eleven millions.

Such was the band of rogues who attached themselves like insatiable vultures to the bosom of Canada and precipitated her ruin. The number of these knaves was further augmented by certain officers of the Colony who had adopted their code of morals. The artillery service was under the command of a Captain Le Mercier, who entered Canada as a common soldier, was schoolmaster during a certain time in the little town of Beauport and became a dangerous intriguer, without talent and without conscience. Landing penniless he had amassed since 1750 a fortune estimated at 700,000 *livres*.

An engineer, without any experience in his profession, M. de Lotbinière, directed the works of fortification in Canada. Artillerist and engineer thought of nothing but to increase their fortunes, finding even a means of profit in prolonging the undertakings of their department, for they were parties, under borrowed names, in all the contracts and reserved for themselves a share of the fraudulent profits in buildings, in the supply of tools, the transportation of materials and also in the sale of brandy and wine to all who worked under their orders.

The Governor General, the Marquis de Vaudreuil, might have been able to bridle this flood of knavery and robbery, but he had not the independence and strength of character to curb it. He preferred to shut his eyes to this corruption, which rose like a tidal wave to his immediate circle, not sparing even his own brother, M. de Rigaud de Vaudreuil, Governor of Montreal. Though his honesty placed him personally beyond suspicion, his culpable weakness nevertheless had the disastrous effect of encouraging the authors of the embezzlements and robberies. Slow in making a decision, often neglecting to take the most elementary precautions, M. de Vaudreuil, was also incapable of dissipating the difficulties of a critical situation, which demanded enormous energy and foresight.

According to the War Commissary Doreil, an honest and faithful critic, he was:

> . . . . . a General who had good and straight intentions, who is amiable, benevolent, easy of access and always officiously kind in civility, but the circumstances and the actual task are too formidable for his head. He has need of a counsellor unbiased by private interests who will inspire him with moral courage.

Unfortunately M. de Vaudreuil made the serious mistake of giving his confidence only to charlatans and knaves. Péan, Lotbinière, Le Mercier, disreputable and unenlightened individuals, were his favourite counsellors. His plans for the campaign were suggested by their interests while often Montcalm only learned the intentions of the Governor from common rumour, or was consulted merely to ward off some immediate clanger. These sinister counsellors were aware M. de Vaudreuil viewed with regret the coming to Canada of a general of the regular army; they encouraged his propensity to favour the Canadians, his compatriots, in all things and everywhere, to the detriment of the French battalions; they skilfully nourished his jealousy of the brilliant officer, who overwhelmed his weakness with the superiority of genius; moreover, they employed every means to conceal from Montcalm the condition of the Colony, its needs, its resources, and to reduce him to an inefficient and mortifying position.

Though they heaped humiliations upon him, nevertheless

Montcalm many times endeavoured to make his voice heard. M. Doreil wrote to the Minister of War, October 22, 1757;

> ...nothing escapes his foresight and his zeal, but what can he do, or can I? Make reports to which they are always antagonistic and which are hardly ever considered.

Tired of the conflict, Montcalm had come to the point of desiring his recall;

> ...from a country where the commander in chief seems only intent upon belittling the share of the regulars and myself in any success and blaming us for any events which prove unfortunate.

One of his first letters, addressed to M. de Crémilles, lieutenant general attached to the Ministry of War by Marshal de Belle-Isle, after recommendations in favour of his officers, contains the expression of his desire to be recalled to Europe:

> What I have most at heart is that the favours I propose for the troops serving under my orders should be granted. I should be very glad to be recalled; that is the greatest favour to be accorded me and my only ambition.

Awaiting a favourable opportunity to place frankly before the Minister of War himself the question of his return to France, Montcalm had too exalted an opinion of his duty as a soldier not to devote himself without reserve to the defence of Canada. More than anyone else, he felt the importance of preserving for the King this beautiful Colony, so rich in its soil, its lakes, its forests, of which the 80,000 inhabitants showed a sincere attachment to the mother country.

> What a Colony! Such a people as one would wish for! What a career is there offered to a Colbert! (he wrote to the Minister of the Navy, the 11th July 1757).....They all have a foundation of intelligence and courage, but up to this time nothing has given life to this body, nor served to develop the seeds which exist.

The Canadians were born soldiers. From the age of sixteen years, they were registered on the rolls of the militia. Boatmen and good shots, hunters inured to fatigue, they excelled in sudden attacks, in forest war and ambushes. Vaudreuil, always prone to praise their services and to attribute to them the success of all our enterprises, too often forgot that the war in Canada had assumed a different character from the impromptu expeditions of the past, accomplished in a few days, where a handful of Canadians and savages were sufficient to put the English to rout. The operations in the New World now compared with those of the wars of Europe, in the importance of the effectives and of the artillery engaged, and by the methodical proceedings of the sieges and the defence of strongholds. These campaigns necessitated operations continuing through many months, to fight in regular formation, to pass from the offensive to the defensive, to give proof of unremitting patience, of "that firm courage," as it used to be called, which the Canadians were far from possessing to the same degree as the regulars.

Unfortunately abuses slipped into the management of the militia and prevented the Colony from deriving all the advantages that it had the right to expect from its services. Without counting the men necessary for the indispensable cultivation of the crops, who had to be left in their parishes, or sent back at harvest time, a large number of militiamen were to be found serving elsewhere than in the army. Montcalm shows clearly in his journal the reason of the small number of militiamen in the army:

Primarily, they summon a certain number of the best kind of the inhabitants to go to war. They register them on the rolls; they equip them appropriately. When they are ready to start, they offer them the choice either to hire themselves at a contemptible wage to go to the Western sea, to the Bay, ere, or to 'march to the firing line.' That is the expression which is used here and one finds it very expressive. Their choice is neither delayed nor doubtful. They hired for the trades and it is reported they are at the

MARQUIS DE VAUDREUIL
Governor-General of Canada. The first
fort at Ticonderoga was named after him

War; the rolls confirm it.

Secondly, the Commissary of Stores has need of people, and in great numbers even, for his transports. Instead of having calculated the number necessary, of having withdrawn them from the militia force as a whole and enlisted them for the campaign, they summon the militiamen for the war; they put them on the rolls of the army; then they exempt them from service, on condition they will make two or three voyages *gratis* for the Commissary. Hence it follows the army seems numerous and in it march actually only the worst type of men, leaving the parishes crippled.

If it were difficult to assemble an army of 3,000 militiamen and to hold them during all the course of a campaign, the savages were also auxiliaries upon whom it was impossible to reckon in operations of a long duration. At the first skirmish, at the first scalp fallen to their tomahawk, they often spoke of returning to their wigwams. One was obliged to use patience with them, to face their tedious councils, to retain them with presents and flattering words, because these inconvenient allies were a precious help, even indispensable, serving as guides and scouts, preventing ambushes, in this country covered with forests and unexplored. From the beginning, Montcalm had been able to understand the capricious personality of these nations ruled by impulse and having a language full of imagery and poetry. He quickly familiarized himself with their manners and customs, adopted their speech and produced such a deep impression on their warriors they believed in listening to him they heard the Manitou of battle. Assured of the confidence of the Canadians and of the savages, the French General felt justified in writing to the Minister of War, the 17th September 1757:

> To the former, when I travel, or in the Camps, I have the appearance of a tribune of the people. The latter have been drawn to me by my successes, which any other might have won; a considerable knowledge of the habits of the savages and the consideration I have shown them.

Montcalm had more reason to depend on the marines in Canada, comprising forty Free companies. These companies numbered only thirty at the opening of 1756, but a royal warrant, of the 14th March 1756, ordered the number to be increased to forty, a thing made possible by the arrival of 1,100 recruits, from whom M. de Vaudreuil subtracted 750 men for the marines. Complete, each company should number 65 men, but in several this figure was not reached. One might be justified in computing the effective of the marines at the beginning of 1758 at 2,200 men. Of great courage, these Free companies, without any permanent ties to one another, gave precedence in discipline and cohesion only to the battalions of regulars.

These last comprised eight battalions belonging to the second battalions of the regiments of Guyenne, Béarn, Languedoc, the Queen, La Sarre and Royal-Roussillon and to the second and third battalions of the Berry regiment. Of these battalions the four first disembarked in Canada in 1755, La Sarre and Royal-Roussillon in 1756, Berry in 1757. Never was a finer spirit shown by any troops than by these battalions on leaving France, and yet Count d'Argenson, Minister of War, had not learned without grave solicitude the decision made by Louis XV, in the beginning of 1755, to send troops of his department to Canada. It was the first time such a considerable body of troops had been detached from the regular army for the defence of distant colonies: to the four battalions of Guyenne, Béarn, Languedoc and the Queen, destined particularly to New France, were joined also two battalions of Artois and of Bourgogne, called to the defence of Louisburg, the capital of Ile-Royal.

In confiding to M. de Crémilles, lieutenant general, the responsibility of supervising the embarkation of these battalions at Brest, d'Argenson had authorized him to supply the number of men who might be wanting to complete the companies with volunteers from the first battalion of each regiment. Fearing even the numbers of these volunteers might not be sufficient, d'Argenson had determined, if necessary, to complete the companies embarked with the men of two battalions of the militia of

LOUIS XV. OF FRANCE

Bretagne (those of Vannes and of Carhaix) placed at the disposal of M. de Crémilles. Following the example of the minister, this general officer expected to have to fulfil a most disagreeable duty. Great was his surprise to witness the enthusiasm shown, the 4th April 1755, by the soldiers of the battalion of Guyenne, the first called upon to embark.

All the officers and soldiers not only showed "much gaiety and an admirable spirit," but, when M. de Crémilles wished to fill out their ranks with soldiers taken from the first battalion, more than three quarters of this battalion asked also "to be permitted to embark, from which it appears, there is not one soldier who does not march of his own free will and who has not offered himself." Three captains, whose plausible reasons for not following their companies were accepted, had been immediately replaced by three officers who volunteered.

Two days afterwards, at the embarkation of the second battalion of Languedoc, M. de Crémilles was wholly occupied in deciding the contests amongst the soldiers of the first battalion "who pressed forward in crowds to join their comrades." On the 8th Aril, the turn of the battalion of Béarn came. Someone had reported this regiment to the minister as having shown little enthusiasm. M. de Crémilles hastened to deny these false rumours.

Without exception all answered the roll call, (he wrote the same day to the Minister of War), and there was no other precaution to be taken, but to prevent the absolute annihilation of the battalion which is not going by the total absorption of its soldiers. Although, your Lordship, the men so far embarked are fine and good, one must acknowledge the 2nd battalion of Béarn surpasses the others by their fine appearance and the height of the men, as well as by the way they are clothed and equipped.

Finally, following the example of the battalions of Bourgogne and of Artois, the battalion of the Queen embarked the last, the 14th April 1755, "with every demonstration of the greatest joy and the most decided enthusiasm." Far from having to make any appeal to the militiamen of the battalions of Vannes and of Carhaix, M. de Crémilles had been witness of a zeal and ardour which rendered his task as easy as it was agreeable. Nor did he spare his praise of the enthusiasm of the entire force embarked.

> There are actually on the vessels of the King, six battalions fully complete in officers and men, amongst whom I do not believe there is one who is not determined to sacrifice his life to maintain the glory and the interests of his master. How pleasing it is for me, your Lordship, to have been the witness and instrument which you have deigned to make use of for the fulfilment of an event which will be forever an infinite honour to the French nation. . . .

Starting with an effective force of 525 men (a company of grenadiers of 45 men, twelve companies of fusiliers of 40 men) the battalions of the Queen, of Languedoc, Béarn and Guyenne, disembarked at Quebec at the end of June 1755. They lost 33 from deaths on the voyage, and two more on arriving at Quebec. Besides, two ships transporting the company of the grenadiers and three companies of fusiliers of each of the battalions of Languedoc and of the Queen, had been captured, the 8th June 1755, by the fleet of Admiral Boscawen, so that the complement of the four battalions, the 25th July 1755, comprised only 118 officers or such like, 1,734 sergeants, grenadiers and fusiliers to whom should be added 135 servants, women and children.

In Canada the enthusiasm of our soldiers did not cool in the least. M. de Malartic, the Adjutant of the Béarn regiment, the 6th October 1755, stated "the soldier had the same spirit that he had at Brest." His evidence was confirmed, the 28th October 1755, by the Commissary of War, Doreil, who wrote to the Minister of War:

> The troops are in the best of spirits; they endure with infinite firmness and zeal the hardships and fatigues to which they have been constantly exposed since their arrival. . . .

An actual proof of this excellent spirit is shown in the fact that at the end of October 1755 no soldier had yet placed himself in the position requiring his appearance before a court-martial and that during the first two years of their sojourn in Canada only one man was convicted by a military tribunal. The Governor, M. de Vaudreuil, joined also in rendering "very favourable testimony as regards the conduct of the battalions of the Queen, of Languedoc, Guyenne and Béarn," having written to this effect to the Minister of War, the 8th June 1756.

As the war in America each day grew in importance and as the regulars had lost their commander, Baron de Dieskau, captured by the English, the court of Versailles caused to be embarked with Montcalm, during the month of March 1756, the second battalions of the regiments of La Sarre and Royal-Roussillon. On their arrival at Brest was witnessed a renewal of the enthusiasm and emulation which distinguished the departure of the first troops sent to Canada. The general, M. de Cursay, charged with completing these two battalions, advised d'Argenson, the 25 March 1756:

> The second battalion of the regiment of La Sarre embarked this morning. It displayed an excessive joy and, if there are soldiers over there who have equally good spirits, one may reckon on the most complete success. There was one officer who gave up his entire fortune to persuade another to retire and cede his place to go to America.

Having assisted at the embarkation of the battalion of La Sarre, Montcalm wrote himself to the Minister of War, the 24th March 1756:

> One can add nothing to the willingness, the appearance of content and gaiety with which officer and man embarked.

Two days later he made the same eulogy of the battalion of Royal-Roussillon:

> . . . . which has just embarked with great enthusiasm, as

much on the part of the officers as of the soldiers. This regiment seemed fine to me, well supplied and well disciplined.

Under Montcalm, from the beginning of their first campaign, the French battalions not only rivalled the Canadians in endurance of cold, of hardship and privations; one saw them also devote themselves, outside of their operations against the enemy, after the example of the Roman Legions, "to various works of fortification and in making good roads, necessary in war time and useful in times of peace." Their general admirably epitomized, in these terms, the detailed services they rendered in the course of two campaigns:

> It is of importance to the service of the King that expatriated troops should be well treated, particularly when they serve with so much zeal and lend themselves to everything: war, labour, stinted food, marches, expeditions in bearskins, winter detachments over the ice.

During the course of the year 1757, new reinforcements arrived for Montcalm: the second and third battalions of the regiment of Berry, at first destined to India, on a footing of nine companies of 60 men to the battalion, embarked at Brest for Canada, in April 1757, numbering 59 officers, 1,033 sergeants, grenadiers and fusiliers, and 26 servants.

Eight companies, raised to replace the eight companies of the regiments of the Queen and of Languedoc, which were captured in 1755, during the voyage of these regiments to America, left France a little later.

The two battalions of Berry arrived at Quebec much exhausted by the voyage, after having left 91 sick at Louisburg and losing 40 dead during the passage. They crowded the hospital at Quebec with more than 200 sick, of whom a great number expired, in spite of the devoted care by which they were surrounded. By the 16th September 1757, they were reduced to 822 men.

The eight companies of recruits, assigned to the regiments of

WILLIAM PITT
Prime Minister of England

the Queen and of Languedoc also arrived much weakened, with a total of 255 men, so that the effective force of the regulars, on the 1st October 1757, amounted only to 3,988 men.

From the 1st November 1756 to the 1st October 1757, the regulars had acquired only 369 recruits arrived from France and 7 recruits obtained in the Colony. Also, far from being able to conform to the warrant of 25th February 1757 which augmented by 10 men the companies of the six battalions of the Queen, La Sarre, Guyenne, Languedoc, Royal-Roussillon and Béarn, Montcalm found himself obliged to carry on these companies of those regiments with an average of 39 men, instead of attaining the number of 50 men.

The recruits who came from France in 1757 were the "collection of a bad lot." The eight companies divided between the regiments of the Queen and of Languedoc comprised in their ranks various rotten elements. Montcalm, to whom the maintenance of discipline was the first consideration, did not hesitate to make numerous examples. During the winter of 1757 to 1758, he caused to be convicted;

> . . . .by ordinary form of law, or by a court-martial, sixteen soldiers of our battalions. Three of them were executed for desertion, two condemned to the Galleys for mutiny against their sergeants and the rest for thieving.

Owing to these severe punishments, as well as the preponderance of the good seed to that of the spoiled, discipline, momentarily relaxed, was re-established. On the other hand, Montcalm could congratulate himself on the understanding which existed between his soldiers and the Canadians and the savages. They are "like brothers" with them, he wrote to the Minister of War, the 18th September 1757. "Our troops," he wrote again in a letter, dated the 18th of April 1758, "live in perfect union with the Canadians and the savages." Our soldiers, very well treated, employ themselves in highly remunerative works, and had "so to speak, too much money." The majority, billeted during the winter amongst the country people, lived in perfect accord with their hosts. In those immense spaces, they breathed an air of independence and of liberty and became more and more attached each day to that marvellous country of which they felt the captivating charm. Guided by views full of wisdom, desirous of working for the prosperity of the Colony, Montcalm encouraged the marriage of his soldiers with the Canadian women.

Eighty marriages took place during the winter of 1756 to 1757, while during the preceding winter one could have counted only seven. Montcalm even demanded of the Minister of War, when His Majesty should come to withdraw his troops from Canada, that He should give "a small bounty to each of His soldiers who then might wish to settle and get married. We would leave the majority: they would make excellent colonists, brave defenders of New France; and, should they return to the kingdom, a severe discipline and less pay would seem to them intolerable."

The number of marriages increased again during the winter of 1757 to 1758, and Montcalm, a clever economist, favoured by every means in his power this transplantation of our soldiers in Canada.

They seem to take a liking to a sojourn in this Colony, (he wrote to the Minister of War, the 18th April 1758). Many marriages continue to be made. Several, without marrying, have this winter acquired land to cultivate and without exempting them from military service, I lend myself willingly to all the arrangements which the political interest of the Colony demands. We could not leave here too many soldiers of our battalions. We should bring them back a scourge to Europe, and we could leave them a benefit to America.

The captains of the eight French battalions had been given commissions of lieutenant colonel on their departure from France, except those of the 3rd battalion of Berry. These officers had performed long and faithful services. M. de Roquemaure, the eldest, had his commission as ensign dating from 1723. Full of zeal, performing his duty with distinction, Montcalm esteemed him. The French general considered the lieutenant colonel of La Sarre battalion, M. de Senezergues, as unparalleled. He appraised him as "a meritorious officer who might aspire to anything and is qualified to be advanced in rank." M. de Senezergues knew how to gain the affection of his subordinates while always preserving amongst them the strictest discipline.

Of the Chevalier de Bernetz, lieutenant colonel in command of the Royal-Roussillon, Montcalm said:

> With courage worthy of his extraction, this officer is very intelligent and well placed at the head of a corps.

The French battalions had also the advantage of having adjutants of great experience and expert in infantry tactics. Montcalm could not exhaust his commendations of the cleverness of M. de la Pause, adjutant of the regiment of Guyenne and of M. de Malartic, adjutant of the regiment of Béarn. They are "two officers of the greatest distinction," two officers "of the highest order," he does not cease to repeat in his letters to the Minister of War. He describes M. de la Pause as an officer "admirable in details," one who conceives "the various operations of the war largely. He understands the principle of superior tactics and has much knowledge of fortification: he is one to find employment on his return on the General Staff of the Army." He goes even to the extreme of calling him "a divine man." M. d'Hert, surnamed Bras de fer, adjutant of the Queen, was also "very good." M. de Joannes of the Languedoc, M. de Bellecombe of the Royal-Roussillon, filled with equal distinction the duties of this rank.

All the grenadier captains were of rare merit and of proved courage. Let it suffice to mention M. de Poulhariès, captain of grenadiers in the Royal-Roussillon, whom Montcalm described as "an officer of the highest distinction fit to be at the head of a corps," and M. d'Alguier, of the battalion of Béarn, "the senior of all those who are here and perhaps of all those remaining in France." Since 1756, he had been recommended by Montcalm for a pension.

"Long service, without other means of support and having suffered a severe wound at the attack of Assiette," he wrote to the Minister of War, "seem to me to justify his claim to obtain it."

Amongst the ordinary captains were to be found many with high qualifications, beginning with M. d'Hebecourt, of the regiment of the Queen, "qualified to rise above mediocrity and who might, continuing his service, hope for promotion owing to his industry and his talents;" Captain Germain of the same regiment, often serving as an Engineer; Captain Pouchot, of the regiment of Béarn, who built Fort Niagara, one of the strongest places of New France, and gained the affection of the savages of the country of the Highlands who surnamed him "the heart of good business;" M. Bernard, captain in the same regiment, an officer "of the greatest willingness;" M. du Prat, captain in the battalion of La Sarre, enlisted in the ranks in 1736 and "one of the few for the remainder of their life devoted to the service;" besides many others, to whom the names of two partisan officers must be added, Lieutenant Wolfe, ex-sergeant of the regiment of Anhalt and Lieutenant Carpentier, ex-sergeant of the regiment of Piémont, both made officers "for distinguished services" before going to Canada, where they continued to deserve the greatest praise.

At the head of the undertakings of the Engineers was M. de Pontleroy, senior captain, appointed in 1757 engineer in chief of New France and remarkable as much for his ability as for his integrity. On arriving at Quebec, M. de Pontleroy had energetically refused to dip into the embezzlements of the Lotbinières and the Le Merciers, They endeavoured also to detain in that city the man whose strict honesty interfered with the plans of so many rogues. Nevertheless, in consequence of Montcalm's repeated demands, M. de Pontleroy managed to take part in the campaign of 1758, where his services proved to be most useful. This engineer was admirably aided by M. Desandrouins, junior captain, who had directed with success the siege works at Chouaguen, in 1756, and at William Henry, in 1757. M. De-

MICHEL CHARTIER, MARQUIS DE LOTBINIERE
Planned Fort Ticonderoga

sandrouins united also to the most perfect integrity a complete knowledge of all branches of the art of fortification. The artillery consisted of two companies of 50 gunners. Leaving out Le Mercier, absorbed more by his own interests than the welfare of the Colony, Montcalm could count upon several officers sent out from France, amongst others MM. de Montbeillard, captain, and de Louvicourt, lieutenant, who by their knowledge, their modesty, and incessant labour, substantiated the glorious traditions of which the Royal Corps had at this period a just claim to be proud.

Among the officers of the personal staff of Montcalm, his three *aides-de-camp* deserve to receive attention.

The best known is M. de Bougainville. Marvellously gifted in the sciences, he had already written at twenty years of age, in 1751, the first volume of his Treatise on integral calculus which procured him the advantage of admission, in 1756, to the Royal Society of London. Lieutenant in the dragoon regiment d'Apchon, in February 1755, Bougainville owed his transfer to America with the rank of captain upon half-pay, to the recommendations of Chevert and M. de Séchilles. Montcalm was not slow in yielding to the charm of the conversation of his young *aide-de-camp*, of his sense and justice, of his enthusiasm in seeking knowledge. After his first campaign in Canada, he drew this flattering picture of him:

> You could hardly believe the resources I find in him. He is well qualified to hold his own. He goes forward willingly to meet gunfire, a matter wherein it is more needful to restrain him than to urge him on. Either I shall be very much mistaken, or he will have a good military head, when experience shall have given him a glimpse of the possibility of difficulties. Meanwhile there is no other young man at present who, versed only theoretically, knows as much as he does.

The following year, Montcalm requested a commission of quartermaster general for the young officer upon whom he depended more and more each day and whom he was to employ later on the important mission to advise Versailles of the real situation in Canada.

Another cavalry officer, M. de Rochebeaucourt, also serving with a commission of captain upon half-pay fulfilled the duties of second *aide-de-camp* to Montcalm. Such was his willingness, he was always ready to march as a volunteer upon the most perilous expeditions. During the campaign of 1759, Montcalm committed to him the responsibility of training 200 volunteer cavalrymen, who, under his able command, were able to serve the army usefully.

The third *aide-de-camp*, Marcel, of a more obscure origin, for a long time a soldier and a sergeant in the regiment of Flanders, had only the commission of Lieutenant upon half-pay in the regiment of the Queen. He served as secretary to Montcalm, never left him and acknowledged, by an unlimited devotion, the kindness of his general to whom he owed all his advancement.

The major general of the small expeditionary corps was the Chevalier de Montreuil. The responsibility was a little heavy for his shoulders; it required a constant activity which perhaps the incumbent did not exercise, but this officer was the model of honour, of courage and of zeal, and Montcalm took many occasions to show his appreciation of his fine qualities.

Finally the two officers who directly supported the French general in the command of our eight battalions, M. de Bourlamaque, as a colonel, and M. de Lévis, as a brigadier, were entirely worthy of his confidence.

M. de Lévis had served a long time in the old regiment of the marines, gaining the esteem of Montcalm, who often fought by his side, in Bohemia and in Italy. He had also, in 1747, fulfilled the duties of adjutant general, under Marshal de Belle-Isle, winning the applause of the army of Provence. A soldier of wide experience and coolness, accurate and deliberate in action, M. de Lévis was not long in gaining the respect of the Canadians and of the savages in the same way he won that of his chief, who said of him in a letter to the Minister of War, dated November

M.LE. VIC.^{TE} DES ANDROUINS

Ch.^r de Malthe Né le 12. x^{br} 1740.

Depute des Baill.^{gs} de Calais et Ardres,

à l'Assemblee Nationale

de 1789.

VICOMTE DES ANDROUINS

Planned the Abatis at Ticonderoga and took
part in the action, July 8, 1758

1, 1756:

M. de Lévis has taken very well with the troops. He has a soldierly manner, the habit of command. He is never at a loss. He knows how to lead, to be discreet in disregarding orders given from a distance of 60 leagues, when he believes them ill-advised owing to circumstances which an absent General could not have anticipated.

To the Minister of the Navy, M. de Moras, Montcalm wrote, the 11th July 1757:

I could not have a better second.

M. de Bourlamaque, son of a captain of grenadiers, of the regiment of the *Dauphin*, killed at the Battle of Parma, entered this regiment as a volunteer in 1739. adjutant in 1745, commissioned captain the same year, he attracted the attention of lieutenant general, the Marquis de Brézé, who remarked in October 1753:

He was well acquainted with this officer prior to the encampment under his command last year, but he did not know his full worth; he had never met any better general officer.

The talents of M. de Bourlamaque designated him in 1755 to assist in revising the regulations for infantry drill. Chevert and the Count de Maillebois soon recommended d'Argenson to send him to Canada and the course of events showed how fortunate this selection was.

In March 1756, commissioned colonel, M. de Bourlamaque had been received with a certain mistrust by Montcalm, to whom he was quite unknown and whom he had at first considered towards the end of 1756, as:

. . . . .not yet having the habit of command, too devoted to details, too letter bound with orders given by a general from a distance of 80 leagues; one who does not speak the language of war.

The campaign of 1757 completely dissipated these prejudices of Montcalm, who corrected his first impressions and addressed to the minister these noble sentiments:

> M. le chevalier de Lévis and M. de Bourlamaque are able seconds in command. The former, indefatigable, courageous, of good soldierly habits. The latter, a man of intelligence, of grasp; after the winter and this campaign he gains immensely in the opinion of everybody. I much desire their promotion, but for me to speak of it would seem to be speaking of my own. . . . Anyway, whether I am made a Lieutenant General or not, there will be the same zeal in the service, the same regard for my Minister, and no consideration as regards me should ever interfere with the promotion of the superior officers who are under my command.

CHAPTER 2

Before the Battle of Carillon

In those times, the rivers and lakes were, so to speak, the only available roads for the armies in Canada. A line of water, almost wholly navigable, offered the means of access from the English colonies to the heart of New France. From New York to Montreal, a distance of less than 150 leagues, this line is indicated by the Hudson River, the Lakes Saint Sacrement and Champlain and the River Richelieu. This natural means of communication requires only three short carries, or transport of boats on the backs of men or animals: one, of some leagues, from the English Fort Lydius, on the Hudson River, to the southern shore of Lake Saint Sacrement; another, of only little more than a league, from the northern point of that lake to the French fort of Carillon.

This latter carry becomes necessary to avoid a bend blocked with rapids in the river by which the Lake Saint Sacrement flows into Lake Champlain, and which the French have named "*rivière de la Chute*" (river of the Fall). From Lake Champlain to the confluence of Richelieu River into the Saint Lawrence, navigation is only interrupted for a moment at Chambly. Naturally the French and English encountered each other on this direct path of invasion and on these undefined frontiers. The English had built a fort to the south of Lake Saint Sacrement, which they named William Henry, and the French, Fort George. It was captured by Montcalm during the campaign of 1757 and destroyed so effectively that the most advanced English post was carried back to Fort Lydius, or Edward, on the Hudson, some leagues to the south of Lake Saint Sacrement.

To bar the road to Montreal to their enemies, the French had as defences: in the first line, at the confluence of the river of the Fall into Lake Champlain, a fort which they named Carillon and which the English called Ticonderoga. A little lower down, at the narrowing of Lake Champlain and on the left bank of the lake, stands fort Saint Frederick. From Carillon to Saint Frederick the lake is so narrow that it is called the Saint Frederick River by the French. Finally these latter had besides, on the Richelieu River, covering the immediate approaches to Montreal, two fortified posts at Saint Jean and Chambly.

Of these works, Carillon, the most important, alone deserves the name of fort. Moreover it was far from being finished and showed serious defects, as one might expect knowing that its construction had been the enterprise and under the direction for three years of M. de Lotbinière, as little versed in the practice of his art, as clever in finding, in the prolongation of the works of fortification, a thousand ways of enriching himself at the expense of the King.

Carillon is built on a peninsula, on the rocky point of a spur commanding three bays: the mouth of Lake Saint Sacrement to the west; the source of Lake Champlain, or the Saint Frederick River to the east and finally a third bay to the south, that of the Two Rocks, leading to the river the French call "*rivière aux Chicots.*" The spur, which terminates at the fort, gradually expanding, extends to the interior of the peninsula: its base 500 fathoms from the fort spreads to a wooded plateau 250 fathoms in extent. It comes close in, with its abrupt slopes to the West, to the river of the Fall, from which it is separated in many places by less than 100 fathoms. On the opposite east side its slope, a little less abrupt, runs at a distance of about 300 fathoms along the Saint Frederick River.

The work was rectangular, the angles being bastioned: the long sides measured only 54 fathoms, the short sides, 29 fathoms. It could not hold more than 300 men at the most. "Its walls are made of squared oak timbers placed one upon another,

ANNE JOSEPH HIPPOLYTE
VICOMTE DE MAURES DE MALARTIC
Wounded at Ticonderoga, July, 1758

bound together by cross beams mortised solidly. It is loop-holed throughout." Two half moons, hardly begun, cover the most exposed fronts, and mask, with their too lofty parapet, the fire from the embrasures of the main work. There were "no moats or counterscarps, covered way, nor glacis." The gun emplacements for the artillery are too narrow and so stupidly placed, those besieged could bring to bear only two pieces opposed to the whole battery of the besiegers. The roofs of the stone buildings, two stories high, built in the centre of the enclosure of the fort, tower above the ramparts.

Bombs and bullets would cause such ravages, from splinters of wood and masonry, as to render both the enclosure and the ramparts untenable. The powder magazine is damp, the cistern fed by muddy and unhealthy water. In short, the defects of this work were so serious, M. de Pontleroy, Chief Engineer of New France, considering the hypothesis wherein he would be called upon to conduct a siege of it, would "require only four to six mortars and two cannon."

The English, without doubt, well knew this fort was "very little able to make a defence." They were informed of the critical situation of the Colony, menaced by famine. They also entertained the hope that Montcalm, reduced to impotence from the want of provisions, would be unable to meet them with an army, until after they had captured Carillon and invaded Canada through Lake Champlain.

The Canadians were not soon to forget the gloomy days of the winter of 1757-1758. Already in the month of July 1757, the people of Quebec saw themselves reduced to four ounces of bread a day. On the 18th September 1757 Montcalm reported to M. de Paulmy:

Provisions fail. The people reduced to a quarter of a pound of bread. Perhaps the ration of the soldier must be reduced again. Little powder. No shoes.

In picturing the sad situation of Canada, in the throes of famine, he pointed out the culpable action of the quartermaster and his association, who were more intent on forwarding wine and brandy than wheat;

> .... there is more profit in the former than in the latter ... Let us cover this matter with a thick veil: it perhaps would interest the leading spirits here.

For the winter quarters, the eight French battalions had been equally divided in the governments of Quebec and Montreal: the Queen, Languedoc and Berry, in the former; Béarn, La Sarre and Royal-Roussillon, in the latter. Except the Queen battalion, in barracks at Quebec, and seven companies of Béarn, billeted on the residents of Montreal, the men were dispersed throughout the country, thus more easily providing for their subsistence.

On the 1st November 1757, it became necessary to reduce the soldiers' ration to a half pound of bread and a quarter pound of peas a day, to 6 pounds of beef and 2 pounds of codfish a week. Even so, at the beginning of December, M. de Vaudreuil, in accord with Montcalm, was obliged to have recourse to horse meat and to modify the soldiers' ration, which thereafter comprised, for eight days, 4 pounds of bread, 2 pounds of peas, 3 pounds of beef, 3 pounds of horse meat and 2 pounds of codfish.

These various reductions were accepted without a murmur at Quebec, where the soldier was in barracks and lived under the eyes of their commanders, Montcalm himself giving the example of a frugal table, served with the same provisions as the garrison. At Montreal, where the soldier was billeted with the inhabitants and where the people showed a great repugnance to horse meat as a food and incited the troops to make the same complaint, there arose "certain difficulties" which were speedily suppressed by the firmness of M. de Lévis. On the 9th of December 1757, being informed the soldiers and even the grenadiers of Béarn refused to accept horse meat at the distribution of provisions, Chevalier de Lévis appeared in person, assembled the grenadiers and the soldiers and addressed them.

He depicted to them the misery of the Colony, the unhappy

lot of the inhabitants of Quebec, since several months reduced to a quarter of a pound of bread; the lamentable distress of 2,000 Acadians, refugees in Canada, who lived only on horse meat and dried codfish, without a morsel of bread. He represented to them they should consider themselves in Canada as in a besieged place, where it was necessary to economize the provisions, appealing to their sentiments of honour and of discipline and succeeded in calming their minds.

No further complaint of the reduction of provisions was made thereafter, and the "day of the Kings" 1758, eight grenadiers of the regiment of Béarn carried to Chevalier de Lévis a dish of horse meat cooked after their fashion, which proved very good. Chevalier de Lévis made these grenadiers breakfast with him and gave them wine and two dishes of horse meat prepared by his own cooks, which they found less palatable than their own. He gave them also four *louis*, so that their company might celebrate "the Kings" and drink to his health.

However sad might be the situation of the soldier, it was indeed a matter of envy in comparison with that of the Canadians and the Acadian refugees. Victims of their love of France, the latter succumbed in great numbers to the ravages of smallpox, engendered by their hardships. At Quebec the people perished "of hunger and misery. Reduced to 2 ounces of bread, they sustained themselves with a little beef; there has been no slaughtering for fifteen days," wrote M. Doreil, on the 16th May 1758. Although free from ice for several weeks, not a single vessel has arrived in the Saint Lawrence from France.

"Under such dreadful circumstances," consternation and despair invaded every heart. At the beginning of May 1758, the distress in the government of Quebec was at its climax and though M. de Vaudreuil possessed no resources to carry on a campaign, seeing that city and the neighbouring parishes were so exhausted, the Governor found himself obliged, the 5th of May, to despatch an order to the regiment of the Queen to quit Quebec and march towards Carillon, "where there is a store of provisions of which only stern necessity excused the use with extreme economy."

On the same day, M. de Bourlamaque was ordered to form squads, or detachments, of the soldiers of Languedoc, or of Berry, who were no longer able to subsist on the inhabitants, and despatch them with the officers to be furnished according to their number, to work on Fort Saint-Jean, provided some provisions may be gathered; or to pass them all to Carillon.

At last, on the 19th of May, the first ships from France, so long and so impatiently awaited, anchored in the harbour of Quebec. A Royal frigate and eight merchant vessels, sailing from Bordeaux, soon followed by five other vessels, brought 12,000 quarters of flour.

Together with distressing reports, such as the defeat at Rosbach, our little army learned the consoling news of the appointment of Marshal de Belle-Isle as Minister of War. The marshal, entirely devoted to the interests of his comrades in arms, enjoyed their esteem and their affection, and Montcalm made himself the echo of the feelings of the officers and soldiers, in writing to his late commander, the 28th May 1758:

> The troops confided to my command and myself have learned with the same satisfaction that the leading man of our military caste, who joins to the ability of a great General the qualities of a statesman and the virtues of a citizen, has been willing to undertake our Ministry.

Owing to the assistance received from France, which brought temporary relief of the famine in Canada, the Marquis de Vaudreuil found himself in a position to undertake his campaign as planned.

He had decided to divide his forces into two parts: one under Montcalm, the other under Chevalier de Lévis.

The former would be charged with the defence of the frontiers of Canada on Lake Saint Sacrement and concentrate under his command the eight battalions of regulars, less 400 detached men, say about 3,000 men, who would be reinforced by 600 marines 500 or 600 militia and some savages.

THE MARQUIS DE LÉVIS
The most distinguished officer with the French
forces after the Marquis de Montcalm.

Chevalier de Lévis, together with M. de Rigaud de Vaudreuil, governor of Montreal, and M. de Longueuil, governor of Three Rivers, was appointed to command a corps of about 2,500 men, composed of the 400 detached men of the regulars, 400 marines, 800 militia and a thousand savages. M. de Vaudreuil had the intention to entrust him with the triple mission to prevent the English from approaching the shores of Lake Ontario by rebuilding the ruined fort of Chouaguen (Oswego); to compel the Five Nations of the Iroquois to take up the hatchet against the English; and to make a diversion, by the Mohawk Valley, as far as Corlar (or Schenectady) to the gates of Albany.

Representatives of the Iroquois Five Nations had given M. de Vaudreuil the assurance they would openly declare themselves against the English, if their Nations were supported by our arms. Too credulous, the Governor of Canada at once put faith in their promise. In reality, these people, whose territories to the south of lake Ontario were constantly ravaged by the belligerents, were making similar promises to the English at the same time. They endeavoured above all to remain neutral, to gain time, awaiting a decisive success of one or the other adversary to range themselves on the side of the victor.

Following out this plan, M. de Vaudreuil, towards the end of May, ordered the eight battalion of regulars to march on Carillon.

The battalion of the Queen, obliged to leave Quebec the 14th May, owing to the scarcity of provisions, had been halted for a short time at Chambly, where orders were received to proceed to Carillon, revictualling on the way at Saint-Jean, where they had stored:

.... for each soldier going up to Carillon subsistence for six days, which he would carry with him, to the extent of a pound of bread a day, one quarter of lard and the same quantity of peas for each ration.

Languedoc and the two battalions of Berry, ordered to march by M. de Vaudreuil the 23rd of May, made but a short halt at

Saint-Jean and, between the 15th and the 20th of June, rejoined the battalion of the Queen at Carillon.

The four battalions distributed in the government of Montreal began to move, the Royal-Roussillon on the 16th of June, Guyenne and La Sarre on the 18th, and Béarn the 20th. They remained in their quarters until the last moment "as much for the reason they were not consuming the rations of the King, as that they were within reach of Carillon in twelve days, in case they were needed."

The Royal-Roussillon arrived at Saint-Jean the 19th June, followed by Guyenne one day later. The two regiments proceeded on the 21st.

The La Sarre arrived at Saint-Jean the 22nd June and continued their march the 23rd, followed in two days by the Béarn regiment.

M. de Bourlamaque, who was ordered to command the troops assembling at Carillon, until the arrival of Montcalm, left Montreal June 12th and arrived at his post the 15th.

It was between the 20th and 25th of June, when Montcalm left Montreal, his departure preceding only by a few days that of Chevalier de Lévis, who was going to the borders of Lake Ontario to assemble his little expeditionary force.

From June 19th, M. de Lévis commanded at Montreal six selected pickets of regulars, about 384 men and 18 officers, of the regiments of La Sarre, Guyenne, Royal-Roussillon, Béarn, Languedoc and Berry. The regiment of the Queen, established already since the beginning of June at Carillon, alone furnished no contingent. Volunteers offered themselves in crowds, officers as well as soldiers, to join this detachment, and M. de Lévis had in M. de Senezergues, the Lieutenant Colonel assigned to him, an excellent second in command.

During these movements of concentration, M. de Vaudreuil and Montcalm received at Montreal important news from Carillon. The partisan Wolfe, accompanied by thirty soldiers and six savages, surprised on the 17th June, on the banks of the river of the Fall, an English party, which they routed, making three pris-

DeBougainvill

LOUIS ANTOINE, COUNT DE BOUGAINVILLE
Served under Montcalm. Wounded at Ticonderoga, July 8, 1758.
Afterwards entered the French Navy and became an Admiral.

oners, one of them an ensign of the 55th regiment of Infantry. From these prisoners they learned the English planned to come to Carillon; their commander, General Abercrombie, was at Fort Lydius:

. . . .with three regiments; those of Abercrombie, Murray and Lord Howe; the Highlanders, and five companies of forest rangers. The Blackney regiment was on its way. They were expecting that of Webb and the Royal American; besides 12,000 militia; and they were going to make an entrenched camp at fort George, and camps to cover convoys and working parties and the constant traffic.

These advices reached Montreal the 19th June, but did not have the effect of disturbing M. de Vaudreuil, who, engrossed in preparations for the expedition of M. de Lévis, persuaded himself the English could not have any offensive design upon the frontier of Lake Saint Sacrement. From the very first, Montcalm had penetrated the real designs of the Governor.

On the 30th May, he wrote to his friend M. de Bourlamaque:

The transport from Chambly very slow. I have often spoken of it and till now *Vox Clamantis in deserto*. After all, is one in a hurry? What does one want? Favouring an expedition in the Canadian manner, *inter nos*, without doubt for brother Rigaud; perhaps for Saint Luc, King of the savages. The people want M. le Chevalier de Lévis, but I think myself there will be no French, or few.

Not daring to give the command of this expedition to his brother, "that man living in the dark and led by the first comer," the Governor associated with him M. de Lévis, upon whose ability he could confidently depend. He had also collected with care the detachments assigned to act under their orders: six selected pickets of regulars; the finest companies of marines; Canadians of the "best kind;" Montrealists, superior in warlike qualities to the militia of the government of Quebec; finally a great majority of the savages who fought with us. Though the diversion planned by M. de Vaudreuil might have the happy result of obliging the English to confront it with part of their forces, it had the serious defect of weakening the small army of Montcalm in the principal theatre of operations, for it absorbed more than a third of the best troops of the Colony. Besides it had the disadvantage of delayed action, M. de Lévis not being able to begin the movement until the early days of July.

Montcalm was not able to leave Montreal until June 24th, having received the Memoranda containing the instructions of the Government only the day before.

M. de Vaudreuil began by declaring he had "conferred with M. le Marquis de Montcalm on the actual situation in the Colony." Counting the eight battalions of regulars, 600 marines, 500 to 600 militia and a train of artillery, he estimated at 5,000 men the forces placed at the disposition of his lieutenant. He charged him to make "as soon as he arrived such offensive demonstrations on this frontier of Lake Saint Sacrement as the circumstances, all things considered, would permit" and ingenuously concluded: these demonstrations, in connection with the diversion of M. de Lévis through the Mohawk Valley, "could not but render the English incapable of acting offensively against either of these two parties."

Then, after having suggested at the opening of his Memorandum, that "independently of the siege of Louisburg, the English had offensive views on the frontier of Lake Saint Sacrement and even on that of La Belle-Rivière," that "the part on the lake Saint Sacrement seems the most threatened," M. de Vaudreuil made an effort at the end of this same Memorandum to prove the English would not undertake any offensive movement in that part, and, while authorizing Montcalm to advance on the enemy and give battle, he placed many obstacles in the way of his liberty of action:

Supposing the English should come to lake Saint Sacrement where the former fort George was situated, their proceeding would be susceptible of two interpretations:

in the first place, we have no reason to believe they have force enough for an offensive movement on this frontier, if it is true, as everything proclaims it to be, they are carrying on their expedition against Louisburg, at the same time as their movements towards Belle-Rivière and to rebuild Chouaguen: secondly, it is much more reasonable to suppose the enemy will undertake a bold demonstration of defence. . . .

If, contrary to all expectation, the enemy proceeds to lay siege to Carillon, it will be for M. de Montcalm to decide to advance to attack them on their march, or on the lake, or to await them in an entrenched camp, or such other position as he may judge most advantageous. We wish only to suggest he should not decide to advance to attack the enemy, unless convinced he has enough savages and Canadians to fight them successfully in the forest. M. le Marquis de Montcalm knows, however much we desire to maintain a large force of savages at Carillon, it happens they withdraw themselves after a foray; he will therefore make every effort to persuade them to remain with him, but, if unsuccessful, he will confine himself to harassing the enemy for the purpose of delaying their march, exercising his judgment to avoid compromising himself by a general and decisive engagement.

On reading this astonishing memorandum, Montcalm was unable to control his indignation and at once made it a point to refute its subtle and contradictory arguments by a memorandum which he enclosed with a letter wherein he urged M. de Vaudreuil to read over and modify his instructions. . . .

It is quite enough, under circumstances which may become so critical, that I should undertake to defend, as far as it is possible for me to do so, the frontier of Lake Saint Sacrement with 4,000 men against very superior forces, without laying upon me the burden of instructions of which the obscurity and contradictions would seem to render me responsible for events which may happen and which we ought to anticipate. I acknowledge the integrity of your intent, but I would not know how to start unless you should send me instructions with all the corrections necessary, as well as indispensable, to preserve the reputation of a general officer who has served for your personal glory with as much zeal as for the defence of the Colony.

In the memorandum enclosed with this letter, Montcalm began by denying the statement of M. de Vaudreuil that he consulted with him on the situation in the Colony, since he never had any knowledge of his plans "except like the people generally, in a vague and indefinite way." He had no difficulty in making it clear that having only received 500 or 600 Canadians, instead of the 1,200 previously promised him, his little army would not exceed 4,000 men. He could not refrain from the expression of his astonishment that the Marquis de Vaudreuil should wish to conceal "from himself alone" the forces of the English in that region (the frontier of Lake Saint Sacrement):

The testimony of the prisoners is too conclusive and uniform, and M. le Marquis de Vaudreuil well knows, notwithstanding the expedition against Louisburg, the English have ten battalions of regular troops, rive companies of wood rangers between Orange and Lydius, and may easily be joined by a great body of militia. (Finally and above all, Montcalm insisted that the Governor should modify the confusing instructions of the last part of his memorandum). M. le Marquis de Vaudreuil seems to contradict himself absolutely in the most important article of his instructions. He begins by relying upon the Marquis de Montcalm to advance on the enemy to give him battle on his march, or on the lake and M. le Marquis de Vaudreuil adds in this same article, that he must not expose himself to a general or decisive action. M. le Marquis de Montcalm would not be able to start, unless M. le Marquis de Vaudreuil should entirely change this article of his

LE MAJOR ROBERT ROGER
Commandant en Chef les Troupes Indiennes au Services des
Americains

MAJOR ROBERT ROGERS
Commanded Rogers' Rangers in French and Indian Wars

instructions, or explain it clearly, because, if the Marquis de Montcalm advances to the attack, there is the engagement and he violates the instructions of M. le Marquis de Vaudreuil. If he should wish to govern himself by the last part, he would be obliged to undertake certain measures which would depend upon circumstances and the time the enemy allowed, for an entrenched camp is not always easy to lay out, nor speedily made, and it would be still better to retire to Saint Frederick than to compromise and shut oneself up in an untenable post. . . .

Yielding to the firm attitude of Montcalm, M. de Vaudreuil consented to sign new instructions, the rough draft having been drawn up by the general himself, which closed with these words:

We rely upon the devotion of M. le Marquis de Montcalm that he would be willing to accept the command of this corps, notwithstanding the critical situation in which he might be placed, owing to the very superior forces of the English. . . . Under these circumstances, M. de Montcalm should seek to be informed of the movements of the enemy, to harass him as much as possible, to obstruct his operations and to avoid a general engagement. We must depend on M. le Marquis de Montcalm to take such action as. is permitted by the small number of his troops, to which the scarcity of provisions has reduced the army we confide to him.

After having succeeded in making the Marquis de Vaudreuil modify his instructions, Montcalm left Montreal on the 24th of June, at five o'clock in the evening, accompanied by M. de Pontleroy, Chief Engineer of New France. The 27th, he met on Lake Champlain "Ignace, Chief of the Hurons of Lorette, despatched by M. de Bourlamaque to report to him the establishment of the enemy at the end of Lake Saint Sacrement on the ruins of Fort George." Several canoes soon followed the Huron Chief, manned by savages, who were conveying to Montreal some English prisoners captured on Lake Saint Sacrement.

These prisoners concurred in reporting the troops of General Abercrombie increased daily at Fort Lydius and that in the English camp it was believed the French, owing to the famine, would not be able to assemble an army. Montcalm encountered also a convoy of boats transporting militiamen of the government of Montreal, who were returning to that city.

They are too good to be left for our use, (he writes ironically in his journal). They belong to the army of favouritism. . . . That chimerical expedition to Corlar (so called by the couriers) will perhaps be the cause of the loss of the Colony.'

With regret Montcalm observed that division of our feeble forces. It would have been better, according to him;

. . . . to advance at once on the enemy with the savages, the choicest of the Canadians, the regulars and colonial troops. They are not yet entrenched; according to the report of the prisoners, they are persuaded the scarcity of provisions has placed us without means to concentrate an army; they are less on their guard and concerned only in completing their works. A sudden attack would overthrow them and finish the campaign at this point. The Marquis de Vaudreuil could then undertake, either to send assistance to the Belle-Rivière or to carry on his intended negotiations with the Five Nations. But who knows whether a decisive success is desirable for this Colony, if a General of the regular army were to achieve it?

As has been said, the courier and the prisoners encountered by Montcalm on his journey had been despatched in all haste to M. de Vaudreuil by M. de Bourlamaque. Since his arrival at Carillon, the 15th of June, M. de Bourlamaque had given a vigorous impulse to the works at the fort, which M. de Lotbinière directed, and he had especially endeavoured to discover the plans of the English and their forces to the south of Lake Saint

Sacrement.

For that purpose he had employed the partisan officer Wolfe, whom he ordered to embark with an escort on the lake, under the pretence of carrying to General Abercrombie letters from Marquis de Vaudreuil, concerning the return of two English officer prisoners, Lieutenant Colonel Schuyler and Captain Martin, who had been authorized to proceed to New York to attend to their affairs. As Lieutenant Wolfe, expected at Carillon on the 23rd June, did not return, M. de Bourlamaque wisely concluded the English held him in their camp to prevent his giving information of their preparations. He also decided to detach M. de Langy-Montégron, naval ensign, at the head of some sixty savages, with the mission to penetrate to the end of the lake, to take prisoners and reconnoitre the movements of the English.

On the 25th June, M. de Langy returned from his reconnoissance. He brought hack with him one officer and fifteen rangers, or *coureurs des bois*, captured on an island two leagues from the end of the lake, where he was able to observe important movements of troops and many boats. It was learned from these prisoners the English intended to march on Carillon:

. . . . in fourteen days to the number of 25,000 men, of whom 6,500 and more were regular troops; that a corps of 7,000 men of this army, under the command of Lord Howe, would proceed by land, the remainder by water, by means of fifteen hundred boats and barges carrying from 25 to 30 men; that they awaited, from day to day, Colonel Johnson with 500 savages of the Five Nations. . . .

Such circumstantial reports did not admit any further doubt of the plan of an English offensive. The 29th of June, M. de Vaudreuil, yielding at last to the evidence, gave Chevalier de Lévis orders to suspend his movement towards Lake Ontario and to turn in all haste to Carillon the first troops of his detachment which were ready to march, that is to say, the pickets of the six regiments concentrated partly at Montreal and partly at Chine. The pickets from Montreal embarked the 1st July, those from Chine the 2nd, descending the Saint Lawrence to proceed by the River Richelieu. Though acting with the greatest promptness, M. de Lévis did not hope to arrive at Carillon before the 10th July, but his energy and the willingness of his soldiers accomplishing prodigies, enabled them to gain two days and permitted them to disembark in time to share the dangers and the glory of their comrades in arms.

On June 30th, at three o'clock in the afternoon, Montcalm, accompanied by his *aides-de-camp*, the Engineers Pontleroy and Desandrouins, made his entrance to Carillon, received with a salute of twelve shots from the cannon of the fort. He found there the eight French battalions, reduced to 2,970 men, "much weakened among themselves on account of the number of worthless recruits and further enfeebled by the pickets of volunteers detached to the Chevalier de Lévis;" 40 marines, 30 Canadians, capable of marching to battle, and 14 savages; provisions for nine days only and in case of urgent necessity, 36,000 cases of biscuit.

With these scanty resources the French general was obliged to meet an imminent attack by the English. The reports furnished Montcalm described the situation as critical:

. . . . the number of the enemy increases daily at the head of Lake Saint Sacrement; their transport is well advanced by a thousand horses and a proportionate number of oxen employed; by the unanimous testimony of the prisoners their plan was to besiege Carillon and to begin their movements during the early days of July; 20,000 to 25,000 men, according to their report, were engaged upon this expedition. . . .

If these reports exaggerated the English forces, it is no less true, at the time Montcalm arrived at Carillon, the enemy had succeeded in concentrating to the south of Lake Saint Sacrement an army of more than 15,000 combatants. The English colonies of North America had spared no means of raising considerable forces and providing for the expenses of an expedition

CAPTURE OF BARON DIESKAU
From an old wood-cut

from which they anticipated decisive results: the invasion and conquest of Canada. Pitt had demanded of them 20,000 men and these contingents were raised under a decree:

> . . . . . published 24th March 1758 in the several colonies of which the following is that for the raising of the contingent from New York: Act to raise, pay and equip 2,680 qualified men, including officers, in order to form, with the forces of adjoining colonies, an army of 20,000 men to invade the French possessions in Canada, conjointly with a corps of His, Majesty's regular troops, and further orders to that effect.

Militiamen of Massachusetts, Connecticut, New York, New Jersey and Rhode Island hastened in crowds to place themselves under the orders of General Abercrombie. According to Parkman, the enthusiasm of these troops was stimulated by their chaplains, who preached a crusade against the abomination of Babylon and compared them already with the soldiers of Joshua, marching against Amalek, cursed of God.

These militiamen numbering 9,000 were to be supported by a strong corps of more than 6,000 regulars belonging to the 27th, 44th, 46th, 55th, and 80th regiments of Infantry, to the Highlanders of the 42nd regiment and to the Royal-American, without counting a detachment of sailors commanded by Lieutenant Colonel Bradstreet and several companies of Rangers, or *coureurs des bois*, under the orders of Major Rogers. For their transport, these troops had at their disposition 900 barks, 135 barges and a great number of flat boats, intended to convey a park of artillery, in sum total nearly 1,500 vessels, which were ready to sail the beginning of July.

The commander of this fine army was Major General Abercrombie, heavy of body and mind, prematurely aged. Political influences had forced his selection by Pitt, but the minister expected the actual conduct of the army would be controlled in reality by an officer having the most brilliant prospects, Brigadier Howe, in whom it pleased him to recognize "a character worthy of the ancients, a perfect model of military courage." Only 34 years of age, endowed with virile energy, Lord Howe had introduced some successful reforms in the army. Under his influence, the officers had divested themselves of all superfluous baggage and had only retained a blanket, a bearskin, a small portmanteau.

"There are no female followers in the camp to do our laundry", wrote an officer under date of June 12, 1758. "Lord Howe has already set an example by going to the creek and washing his own." Abercrombie submitted to the ascendency of his lieutenant; he recognized in him a leader of men, the regulars and the provincials realized in him as well, the soul of the army.

While the English were putting the last touches to the preparation for their embarkation, Montcalm reviewed with coolness the dangers of his situation and adopted prompt measures to avoid them. He knew too well the importance of Carillon, "the key of navigation and consequently of the country," to abandon it without fighting the enemy. "Activity and audacity are our only resources," he writes in his journal under date of July 1st, and this same day, in spite of the disproportion of his forces, he did not hesitate to leave the protection of the cannon of Carillon and occupy the north shore of Lake Saint Sacrement, the carry where the English would probably disembark. By this movement in advance, he hoped to impress the enemy and delay their approach for a few days, time sufficient to enable M. de Vaudreuil to furnish the reinforcements the hazardous situation demanded.

On the 1st July, at half past five in the morning, his little army, divided in three brigades, began its march. The Queen brigade, composed of the regiments of the Queen, Guyenne and Béarn, under the command of M. de Bourlamaque, occupied the head of the carry, at the northern extremity of Lake Saint Sacrement. A half a league in the rear, the Royal-Roussillon brigade, composed of the Royal-Roussillon and the 2nd battalion of the Berry, established itself on the right bank of the river of the Fall, near a sawmill, three quarters of a league distant

FROM AN ENGLISH MAP OF LAKE GEORGE—1758

from Carillon. The La Sarre brigade, composed of La Sarre and Languedoc, rested on the left bank of the river of the Fall, in the neighbourhood of the mill. The 3rd battalion of Berry alone remained encamped by the fort to constitute the garrison in case of an attack.

It was not Montcalm's plan to establish himself on the shores of Lake Saint Sacrement, at the camp at the carry, and to oppose the disembarkment of the English with all his forces, because the position did not favour it. Just as he suggested to M. de Vaudreuil, in his memorandum of June 23rd, "the post at the Carry is at the bottom of a cup from which the enemy would easily drive us, with his superior forces whenever he wished to." For this reason, Montcalm wisely limited himself to preventing the enemy from seizing the Carry "suddenly, as they might do in ten or twelve hours by an advance on the lake," and his object might have been effected probably by the occupation by one brigade of the northern shore of Lake Saint Sacrement.

While the battalions were taking their new positions, Montcalm, accompanied by several officers, amongst others MM. de Pontleroy and Desandrouins, reconnoitred a position indicated by M. de Bourlamaque as fitting to protect the peninsula of Carillon. This position was flanked on the right by a swampy creek flowing into the Saint Frederick River and, on the left, by an escarpment bordering the river of the Fall. It was adjudged excellent for defence, but too distant from the fort to be supplied daily with provisions or to be properly supported; finally and above all, being of too considerable a development for the small number of our battalions.

During the afternoon, MM. de Pontleroy and Desandrouins, ordered to designate a position of less extent and nearer to Carillon, found it at the base of the spur which ended at the fort and at 500 fathoms only from the latter. The development of this new entrenchment was not to exceed a front of 300 fathoms; resting on the flanks on the escarpments of the spur, it could be constructed rapidly by a trench, the earth from which, thrown from the side of the defenders, would form the parapet.

The two Engineers projected also to reinforce this parapet with the trunks of trees, lying in the sense of their length, which the forests in the immediate vicinity of the entrenchment would supply.

The selection of this latter position met the approval of Montcalm and the two Engineers began on the 2nd July "to lay out and picket the entrenchments. Desandrouins corrected everything with a compass."

One hundred Canadians or marines, escorting some boats loaded with 30,000 rations of provisions, arrived at Carillon the evening of the 1st of July. This additional supply of provisions assured the subsistence of our little army until the 16th or 17th of July. Anxious to economize his feeble resources, Montcalm fixed the daily ration of the soldier at a pound and a half of bread, half a pound of bacon and a half pound of peas.

> Officers had one pound of bread and his servant the same. The officer had besides a measure of brandy. The officers had less bread, because they had other provisions than those of the rank and file. This is quite reasonable and should be endured without remonstrance, in the situation in which we are placed, (Desandrouins wrote in his journal).

The troops passed the day July 1st in settling themselves in their camps and completing the transport of their equipment. At night, about 7 o'clock, M. de Bourlamaque despatched two barges, manned by 30 men, to reconnoitre on Lake Saint Sacrement.

To supply the lacking Canadians and savages, Montcalm gave orders, the 2nd July, to form a company of volunteers in each of the camps at the Fall and the Carry. The first was commanded by M. Duprat, captain in the La Sarre regiment; the second by M. Bernard, Captain in the Béarn regiment. Personally, Montcalm established himself in the Fall camp "to be nearer the head of the Carry and the movements of the enemy."

An alarm of short duration took place the morning of the

2nd July, when the report of two shots, fired from an advanced post of the Queen regiment, called to arms the troops of M. de Bourlamaque, until the captain commanding this post had sent word:

> . . . . .to explain that his lieutenant, detached in advance with six men, in seeking his hunting knife, discovered a feather and had promptly jumped behind a tree to avoid a gun shot fired at him by a savage who was ready to rush him, tomahawk in hand, had he not been prevented by coming under fire; that the savage avoided his shot by throwing himself prostrate on the ground and only took flight when the officer shouted: 'To the rescue, volunteers!'

On July 3rd, Montcalm received a reinforcement of 80 Canadians and 30 marines under M. de Raymond, naval Captain. M. Le Mercier also arrived to take command of the artillery and delivered to Montcalm letters from Marquis de Vaudreuil, advising him of the abandonment of the Corlar expedition and the early arrival of M. de Lévis.

During the day July 4th, M. de Bourlamaque employed his troops building a bakery and throwing a bridge over the river Fall, in the vicinity of the first rapid at the outlet of Lake Saint Sacrement. He also had laid out a redoubt to defend this bridge. On his side, Montcalm ordered a bridge to be thrown over the same river, near the saw mill, to facilitate communication between the two brigades of La Sarre and Royal-Roussillon, who were still working to make facings and palisades necessary to strengthen the defence of Carillon.

During the evening of July 4th, M. de Raymond rejoined M. de Bourlamaque with his detachment, and M. de Langy-Montégron, naval ensign, embarked on lake Saint Sacrement at the head of a little reconnoitring flotilla manned by about 150 men "of whom 104 were of our battalions, 25 Canadians and about 20 savages." The emulation was so great amongst our officers that a captain and seven lieutenants marched as volunteers under the orders of M. de Langy, although he was their junior.

Some of the canoes of M. de Langy returned to the Carry on the 5th of July, about 3 o'clock in the afternoon, reporting the end of Lake Saint Sacrement covered with a large flotilla from which 60 barges were detached to give chase to them; that M. de Langy resolutely had opposed his boat alone to meet the enemy, who, surprised by this brave manoeuvre, fearing some trap, slackened their pursuit and gave our canoes the time to escape from their sight; further that M. de Langy remained on the lake to keep in touch with the enemy, of whom these barges were probable the advance guard.

On this information, M. de Bourlamaque at once despatched under the command of M. de Trépezec, a Béarn captain, a detachment composed of three pickets of the Queen, Béarn and Guyenne, volunteers, marines and Canadians, numbering about 300 men. They were ordered to seize a mountain, called Mount Pelée, 3 leagues distant from the camp of the Carry and on the left shore of Lake Saint Sacrement, with the mission to reconnoitre the movements of the enemy and obstruct their landing at this point. M. de Bourlamaque further entrusted three pickets to M. Germain, captain in the regiment of the Queen, to watch over the shores of the lake and the Carry camp and support the advance guards.

Returning to the north shore of Lake Saint Sacrement at about 5 o'clock in the evening, M. de Langy confirmed to M. de Bourlamaque the report of the approach of the enemy and immediately offered to rejoin M. de Trépezec and serve him as guide in that difficult and densely wooded country.

Montcalm, for his part, ordered all the troops "to hold themselves on the alert," to pass the night in bivouac and to begin to clear away their equipment. By his order, the volunteers of Captain Duprat were sent to the little Bernetz River, flowing to the left of that of the Fall; it flowed into the latter at half the distance between the bridge of the Carry and that of the saw mill. As it was fordable in several places the enemy might cross it, once disembarked, to reach Carillon by following the left bank

Croquis donnant la position des troupes de Montcalm le 5 Juillet 1758 dans la soirée.

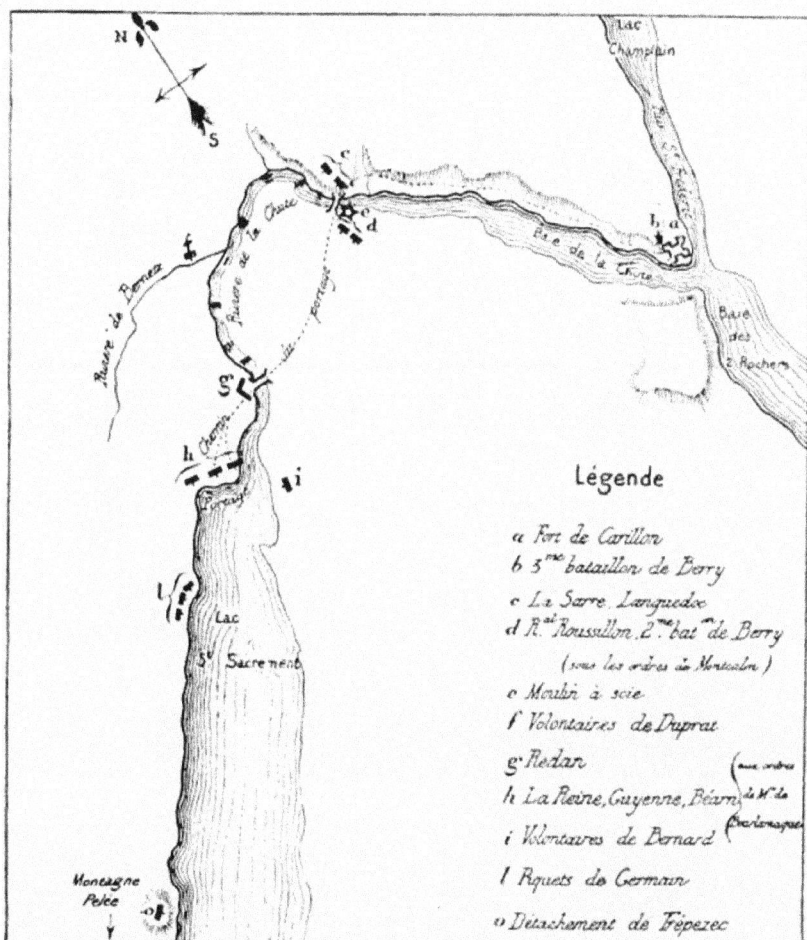

Légende

a Fort de Carillon
b 3.me bataillon de Berry
c La Sarre, Languedoc
d R.^{al} Roussillon 2.me bat.^{on} de Berry
   (sous les ordres de Montcalm)
e Moulin à scie
f Volontaires de Duprat
g Redan
h La Reine, Guyenne, Béarn
i Volontaires de Bernard
l Piquets de Germain
o Détachement de Trépezec

Montcalm au Combat de Carillon (8 Juillet 1758)

Échelle d'une Lieue

PLAN OF ABERCROMBIE'S ATTACK

of the Fall River.

One hundred and fifty Canadians and marines arrived at Carillon during the night of the 5th under the command of three captains, MM. de la Naudière, de Saint-Ours and de Gaspé.

Thus, as M. de Langy had foretold, the arrival of the English fleet was now only a question of hours. During the evening of the 4th July, Abercrombie had successfully embarked his artillery, his munitions, his baggage and his provisions. The 5th at dawn the army set sail, numbering 6,367 regulars and 9,024 militia. Officers and soldiers were filled with perfect confidence in the success of the expedition upon seeing the powerful fleet which covered with its vessels the whole extent of the lake:

> The splendour of that summer day; the romantic beauty of the scene: the sparkling glitter of those crystal waters; the innumerable islands, covered with clumps of pine, birch and fir trees; the neighbouring mountains with their verdant summits and their rocks reflecting the sunshine; the flashes of the oars and the sparkle of the accoutrements; the banners, the various uniforms, the notes of the bugle, the trumpet, the bagpipe and the drum, repeated and prolonged through the woods by hundreds of echoes, (all contributed to make of this scene a picture of enchantment).

The advance guard was composed of the wood rangers of Major Rogers, the light infantry of Colonel Gage and the sailors under Lieutenant Colonel Bradstreet. The main body followed in three columns, the centre composed of regulars in red coats, Lord Howe and his regiment, the 55th Infantry, leading; the wings of militia in blue coats. Following the columns, the boats loaded with provisions and baggage and the heavy flat boats bearing the artillery, formed a special division under the protection of a rear guard composed of militia and regulars.

By 5 o'clock, the fleet had crossed three quarters of the lake. It came to a halt until 10 o'clock to await the boats of the last division which had more slowly advanced, then proceeded and arrived at dawn the 6th of July in sight of the north shore of lake Saint Sacrement.

Lord Howe, Lieutenant Colonel Bradstreet and Major Rogers[1] went together to reconnoitre the landings at the Carry. Discovering only a weak French detachment, they reported immediately to Abercrombie there would be no opposition to his landing.

About 9 o'clock the British army took possession of the Carry. Its general, hoping to invest Carillon the same day by the left bank of the Fall River, formed his troops in four columns, two of regulars in the centre and two of militia in the wings, moving forward as soon as the formation was complete.

Abercrombie had not realized the difficulties to be met in a country covered with a thick virgin forest, through which it was necessary to chop out a road. Having no outlook, advancing over uneven ground little known to their guides, it was not long before the columns were broken and commingled. After a disordered march, long and exhausting, the British Army had advanced but little and had not yet reached the banks of the Bernetz River at 4 o'clock in the evening.

On the French side, the night of July 5th to 6th passed without other alarm at the advanced post of Captain Germain, than a little musketry fire exchanged with a party of scouts landed by the enemy who unsuccessfully endeavoured to capture a corporal and the relief sentinels accompanying him.

At dawn, on perceiving the English fleet, M. de Bourlamaque began the evacuation of his impedimenta which he had purposely delayed fearing such action "might give the impression of timidity." By 7 o'clock, he was rejoined by the pickets of M, de Germain, who fired in passing upon some of the barges of the enemy and had relieved all the advanced posts held by his grenadiers. After having delayed his departure until 8 o'clock in the hope of seeing the detachment of M. de Trépezec appear, he began the movement in retreat on the camp of the Fall, burn-

1. Two books written by Robert Rogers *Journals of Robert Rogers of the Rangers* and *Journals of the Siege of Detroit* also published by Leonaur.

ing some few stores which had not then been removed and destroying the bridge near the first rapid of the river. In complete order and without the loss of a man, the Queen, Guyenne and Béarn, rejoined Royal-Roussillon and the 2nd battalion of Berry. Montcalm then withdrew the two brigades of the Queen and Royal-Roussillon on the left bank of Fall River and destroyed the bridge built near the saw mill. After being joined by La Sarre and Languedoc, the five battalions encamped on the heights near the mill.

While this movement to the rear was being carried out, MM. de Pontleroy and Desandrouins, as early as 7 o'clock in the morning, began to put in a state of defence the position selected by them the 1st of July, and, though they had only 100 workmen of the 3rd battalion of Berry, they took advantage of this day to lay out an entrenchment and study the ground and to decide upon the work for the next day.

The day of the 6th July would have passed without accident to the French if the detachments of M. de Trépezec had been able to rejoin M. de Bourlamaque or Montcalm, but, its line of retreat being cut, this detachment lost itself in the forest. M. de Langy, who was the guide, led them astray notwithstanding his knowledge of the ground. The few savages Montcalm was able to furnish him, had deserted during the march. Towards 4 o'clock in the afternoon, M. de Trépezec had only reached the banks of Fall River, near the confluence of the Bernetz River, unsuspecting the presence nearby of the English columns, continuing laboriously to make a way through the almost insurmountable obstacles of the forest.

With Major Putnam and 200 Wood Rangers, Lord Howe marched at the head of the column on the right of the regulars, when suddenly they heard the challenge, "*Qui vive?*"

"*Français!*" replied the English, though without deceiving their adversaries, who replied with a deadly volley. Lord Howe fell, mortally wounded; the column following him wavered a moment, on the point in dispersing, but the firm stand of the wood rangers gave them time to recover, when the French detachment, overwhelmed by superior forces, saw themselves compelled, after a vigorous resistance, mostly to surrender. One hundred and forty-eight prisoners, including several officers, remained in the hands of the English. About 50 Frenchmen lost their lives in this fight, and only about 100 succeeded in escaping and rejoined Montcalm carrying M. de Trépezec mortally wounded and M. de Langy slightly touched. The English suffered less in the conflict, but the death of Lord Howe was an irreparable loss to them. Contemporaneously Major Thomas Mante wrote:

> It seemed the soul of the army of General Abercrombie expired at the death of Lord Howe. From the disastrous moment when the General was deprived of his advice order and discipline were no longer observed and a strange infatuation usurped the place of determination.

The consequences of this fatal loss were soon to make themselves felt. The whole army uselessly remained the entire night under arms in the midst of the forest. At dawn, as the troops were already very tired by the lake crossing, by their laborious inarch through the forest, and by the want of provisions, "having been obliged to throw away those they had brought with them to relieve themselves," Abercrombie gave the order to return to the shore of Lake Saint Sacrement, the place where they had disembarked, and there they arrived on the 7th July at about 8 o'clock in the morning.

Montcalm with joy watched the enemy making the mistake of throwing themselves across a forest which was like an impenetrable veil and marching towards the Bernetz River, instead of reconstructing M. de Bourlamaque's bridge and marching straight on the camp of the Fall, following the easy road of the Carry. By this false manoeuvre, the English lost a whole day and gave Montcalm a respite of incalculable importance for the arrival of nearby reinforcements and the completion of an entrenched position. Without knowing of the death of Lord Howe, Montcalm, watching the movements of the enemy, was able to

Embarking at the head of Lake George of Abercrombie's expedition against Fort Ticonderoga, July 5, 1758

observe signs of trouble and confusion. He fortunately felt by intuition that a fatal blindness governed their councils and the same evening he wrote to his friend, the Commissioner Doreil, these prophetic lines which do the greatest honour to the perspicacity of his judgement:

> I have opposed to me a formidable army. Nevertheless there is nothing to make me despair. I have good troops. From the movements of the enemy, I see he is vacillating. If by his procrastination, he gives me the time to reach the position I have chosen on the heights of Carillon and to entrench myself, I will vanquish him.

The 6th of July at 5 130 o'clock in the evening, being warned by the volunteers of Duprat, that the enemy was pushing ahead towards the Bernetz River, Montcalm ordered his little army to retire on Carillon. It arrived at 7 o'clock and bivouacked for the night. A reinforcement of 183 Canadians and marines, under a Captain M. de Cannes, arrived to partly make up the loss suffered by our battalions in consequence of the defeat of the detachment of M. de Trépezec.

Chapter 3

The Battle of Carillon

At 3 o'clock in the morning, July 7th, in a reconnoissance of the lines of the entrenchments, MM. de Pontleroy and Desandrouins served as guides to the superior officers of the Queen, Béarn, Guyenne, Royal-Roussillon, Languedoc, La Sarre and the 2nd battalion of Berry (the 3rd remaining to garrison the fort). One hundred and twenty-seven paces were apportioned to each battalion. The entrenchment, rock bound, followed the windings of the ground. Its front had a development of 300 fathoms, to which must be added a return of 150 fathoms, along the escarpment on the right and another of 60 fathoms, along the left escarpment.

Towards 5 o'clock the battalions occupied the positions assigned to them. Whilst companies of grenadiers and volunteers advanced to cover the workers, the latter planted their flags on the works and laboured most willingly, some digging a moat; others felling trees on the border of the forest, only 100 fathoms distant, and dragging them by hand to the entrenchment, leaving the stumps and the branches to obstruct the approach of the enemy. "The officers themselves, axe in hand, set the example."

Montcalm passed along the lines, encouraging the workers and sharing with them the good humour and confidence they read on his face. The Engineers de Pontleroy and Desandrouins "were busy stimulating the soldier at work, in teaching the way to lay the trees and the branches and above all to make the old soldiers appreciate the excellence of the position, protected on

The "Black Watch" at Ticonderoga, July 8, 1758

the two wings by escarpments and having a front of only 300 fathoms. They listened very attentively to the latter exposition and gained confidence."

Thanks to the energy of everyone, the entrenchment grew as by enchantment.

"The army worked with such incredible ardour," wrote Montcalm in his journal, "that the line was in a state of defence the same evening." Only traverses to protect them from enfilade fire were lacking. The parapet was formed of the trunks of trees and the earth from the excavation of the moat. Beyond the latter, important additional means of defence were added by placing trees perpendicularly to the excavation, "of which the branches trimmed and sharpened produced the effect of a *chevaux de frise.*"

The opening, 80 fathoms wide, which extended from the escarpment on the left to the river of the Fall, was barred by cutting, the defence of which was entrusted to the volunteer companies of Duprat and Bernard. This cutting, situated in the left return of the entrenchment, was flanked advantageously by it.

In the plain, 300 to 500 fathoms wide, partially cleared of trees, which extended from the right escarpment to the River Saint Frederick, an abatis had also been begun. The defence (if this abatis, lying in the rear of the right return of the entrenchment and under the protection of the guns of the fort, was entrusted to 450 Canadians and marines, the only reinforcements Montcalm had received up to this time since his arrival at Carillon, when, on the evening of the 7th, between 6 and 8 o'clock, our battalions greeted with their shouts the arrival of the six pickets of M. de Lévis who had "made the utmost speed, advancing day and night, in spite of contrary winds, to rejoin their comrades, knowing they were about to be attacked immediately. Our little army received them with the same joy as the legions of Labienus also met with from the Roman *cohorts* under Quintus Cicero, besieged by a swarm of Gauls."

It was M. Pouchot, captain in the Béarn regiment, who led the first picket landed at Carillon. Being informed of the approach of the English on meeting couriers despatched by Montcalm to M. de Vaudreuil, M. Pouchot, on the 6th, had allowed his troops only four hours' rest, after having spent twenty-four hours rowing on lake Champlain, owing to a contrary wind. They none the less joyously set out on the 7th at the first streak of dawn, oblivious to their fatigue and having only one preoccupation, to arrive in time for the battle.

If the pickets of M. de Lévis were acclaimed with joy, they as well experienced a feeling of surprise and admiration on rejoining our battalions to find "a plan of entrenchments well designed to suit the nature of the ground and a prodigious work." On the other hand, the presence of these officers and picked soldiers completely dissipated the discouraging impression which the defeat of M. de Trépezec might have produced in some minds, and this result was so much the more easily accepted when the new arrivals announced the proximate landing of MM. de Lévis and Senezergues who were following them at a few hours' distance. Chevalier de Lévis, adored by the troops, himself alone was a precious reinforcement of which Montcalm better than anyone else knew the value.

During the day of the 7th, our volunteer companies had perfectly informed Montcalm of the movements of the English. Through them, he became aware the enemy had arrived in force to occupy our late camp of the Fall, on the left bank of the river, less than three quarters of a league from Carillon. Abercrombie, recognizing his error of the preceding day, had decided to follow the easier road of the Carry and during the morning of the 7th, ordered Lieutenant Colonel Bradstreet, with the 44th regiment, 6 companies of the 1st battalion of the Royal-American, the marines and a corps of woodsmen and the militia of the provinces, to occupy the saw mill.

Towards midday Colonel Bradstreet had accomplished his mission without resistance and rebuilt the bridge destroyed by the French the day before. Leaving only a small detachment to protect his boats, Abercrombie joined his advance guard and established himself on the left bank of the Fall River. He also caused to be carried forward several large boats and pontoons, mounted with two cannons, in the hope they would aid in the attack which he intended to direct by land against the position of his adversary.

In consequence of these preparations, Montcalm no longer doubted he would be attacked the following day. Notwithstanding the inequality of numbers, he saw this hour draw near without misgiving, because the strength of his position, joined to the valour of his troops, permitted him now to hope for a happy issue of the battle on which the destiny of Canada was staked.

On the evening of the 7th, Montcalm directed the orders, drawn by a master hand, to he read to the troops setting forth his instructions for the defence of the entrenchments:

Long live the King!

The troops will encamp within reach of their entrenchments. The companies being small, they will camp in two tents for each company. For the officers, there will be a third for each company. Every senior officer will attend to the discovery of creeks or springs, which may be to the rear of the camp, to supply the soldiers with water. The grenadiers will occupy their camp at nightfall. The pickets will be withdrawn and will post themselves on the edge of the entrenchment, throwing out sentinels in advance. . . .

The Canadians and colonial troops will observe closely whatever happens on the right in the hollow of which they have the defence.

Officers and soldiers will sleep in their tents, completely dressed. . . .

When the seven battalions assemble fully armed at dawn, orders will be given for the work to be done to-morrow. Soldiers employed upon useful labours, as bakers, armourers, must necessarily continue. They are required for the service and equally serve the King. . . .

The troops will be pleased to learn M. de Lévis will be here tomorrow and that within three days there will arrive a reinforcement of 300 men and 300 savages. Therefore it is only a question of confidence, courage and steadfastness. M. le Marquis de Montcalm expects that of his troops and promises to obtain for them all the rewards and advantages due to efficient service.

The soldiers cannot be too strictly warned that the great fault of the regulars lies in hasty firing without aim; the result is ammunition is speedily exhausted and that, the enemy continuing to fire, the soldier becomes discouraged. The officers will develop this important matter, which cannot be too often repeated. They will see to it the soldier fires slowly and they must urge him to take good aim. . . .

The battalions will form the line of battle at the first alarm. When they are formed, the companies of grenadiers and the pickets will remain halted, but the battalions will advance and occupy the trenches. They will place somewhat heavier ranks of soldiers at the angles flanked by the redoubts.

The volunteers will place themselves at the issues or exits of the entrenchments to make sallies when the order to do so is given them.

The companies of grenadiers will advance, in case it is required, to the support of the detachment of their battalion, where they see the enemy making progress and will make sallies, if so ordered.

The battalions not engaged will give the support of their grenadiers and pickets to those too vigorously pressed.

The Canadians, camped in the hollow or lower level, will advance, scattering behind the trees, in support of that part; and if they find it necessary to retire, thev will retire to the rear, bearing however somewhat to the right of the Queen regiment.

Battalion Commanders will make use of their judgment and experience in circumstances which cannot be foreseen.

It is of the greatest importance to hold the entrenchments

to the last extremity.

When any order is to be passed during the attack or any requisition made, they are to be carried only by an officer whom each commander of a battalion will send for that purpose.

It is forbidden to make any requisition by word of mouth.

Each commander will have an officer aide.

Each brigade will send an orderly officer, at the beginning of the action, to M. le Marquis de Montcalm.

Ammunition will be served to each battalion.

M. de Bourlamaque is in command of the right.

Guards will be posted tomorrow morning in front of the entrenchments, at 150 paces from the abatis. At night very frequent patrols will be made and silent signals given.

The guards of the camp will be posted on the border of the entrenchments, at the middle of each battalion.

M. de Bourlamaque will order the number of detachments outside.

The arrival of M. de Lévis caused only slight changes in these arrangements. Montcalm reserved for him the special command of the right, leaving to M. de Bourlamaque that of the left and keeping for himself that of the centre.

On the 8th July, by 5 o'clock in the morning, the troops, covered by the ordinary guards and three companies of grenadiers, had taken their battle positions, in the following order: the Canadians and the marines on the extreme right, behind the abatis of the deep hollow; the Queen, Béarn and Guyenne behind the right of the entrenchment; the Royal-Roussillon, the 2nd battalion of Berry and four of the pickets which arrived the day before with M. de Lévis, in the centre; the two remaining pickets of M. de Lévis, Languedoc and La Sarre, on the left; the companies of volunteers of Bernard and Duprat protecting the cutting of the hollow, at the extreme left. Each battalion should have behind it, in line of battle and ready to give support, its company of grenadiers and a picket. The 3rd battalion of Berry, left to garrison the fort, had for its special mission to assure the supply of ammunition to the combatants. Only its company of grenadiers had been summoned to the line of fire and stationed in reserve at the centre.

The total effective force of Montcalm's little army amounted only to 3,500 combatants.

Under the protection of the advanced guards, the battalions worked to complete the entrenchments. Montcalm even contemplated establishing a battery of six pieces 150 or 200 fathoms in the rear of the Duprat and de Bernard volunteers, but his adversary gave him no time to finish this work.

About 10 o'clock in the morning, a detachment of the enemy, composed of light troops and savages, appeared on the right bank of the Fall River crowning the summit of a mountain whence they could view our entrenchments from the rear. The chief engineer of the English army, Mister Clerck, accompanied this reconnoissance. The enemy began a futile exchange of shots with our volunteer companies posted on the opposite bank, but, as most of the bullets fell into the river, our troops ceased firing and continued their work.

The savages belonged to the Iroquois Five Nations. They had arrived the day before, numbering 500, led by Colonel Johnson, the same officer who had captured M. de Dieskau in 1755. After having taken part in this skirmish, they were obliged to be content to remain as spectators of the events of the day behind the English army.

Abercrombie was aware, from the reports of the prisoners of the detachment of M. de Trépezec, that Montcalm, from hour to hour, was expecting reinforcements of marines, Canadians and savages. Eager to forestall the arrival of these reinforcements and not to give time to his adversary to complete his works, the English General had ordered Clerck to find out if an attack on the French entrenchments appeared feasible. Upon receiving a favourable reply from the Engineer and without awaiting his artillery, Abercrombie ordered his army forward. He left but one regiment of militia in the camp of the Fall and moved forward

GENERAL ISRAEL PUTNAM
Served under Major Robert Rogers,
at Ticonderoga

with more than 13,000 men.

A curtain of sharpshooters, made up of selected marksmen, of light infantry and wood rangers, preceded the army which debouched from the forest, about twelve thirty, opposite our entrenchments. It was formed in four columns, pickets and grenadiers leading.

At the approach of the enemy, our advanced guards withdrew in good order. At a cannon shot from the fort, serving as a signal, the workers threw down their tools to retake their place in the battalions which manned the parapet of the entrenchment, three ranks deep, after leaving their pickets and their grenadiers in reserve to the rear.

Montcalm, coatless on account of the heat, was stationed at the centre, having beside him M. de Montreuil, Major General, M. de Bougainville, since three days appointed to the duties of adjutant general, MM. de la Rochebeaucourt and Marcel, his *aides-de-camp*, also M. Desandrouins, who, his duty as engineer finished, had begged the honour of being attached to the person of his general during the battle.

Abercrombie had ordered his troops to "advance rapidly, to throw themselves forward in the midst of the enemy's fire, but to reserve their own, until the works themselves were actually entered." While the right column of the English attempted to turn the left of our entrenchments and came under the fire of the La Sarre regiment, another column attacked the salients of the line between the Languedoc and Berry. A third column was directed against the centre, opposite the Royal-Roussillon and Guyenne. And the left column assaulted the front manned by the Béarn and Queen.

Before reaching the abatis, the English columns were received with a murderous fire. The sections leading, halted and opened fire themselves, and, under the cover of this discharge and that of the selected sharpshooters who "hidden behind stumps and trunks of trees crowded the intervals and wings of the columns," the troops which followed them made repeated assaults on the abatis, but "our musketry fire was so well aimed the enemy was destroyed as soon as they appeared." The vigorous attacks of the assailants were repulsed on every side by the sustained and well aimed fire of the defenders. According to the instructions of Montcalm, our soldiers were allowed to fire at will, a manner of firing at which the French excelled. The officers confined themselves to supervising the direction of this fire and the expenditure of ammunition. During all the battle, their task was facilitated "by the courage of the troops, who devoted their whole attention to firing properly and getting a good aim at whoever showed himself."

> Impossible, (wrote the Engineer Desandrouins), to find greater coolness and courage than one witnessed that day in the soldier. I can testify not one of them fired without singling out his man and that the most of them frequently waited some time until a sharpshooter, posted behind a stump, fairly exposed himself, so as not to miss him, though bullets were raining about them like hail.

Montcalm and his lieutenants, MM. de Lévis and de Bourlamaque, watching the course of the battle, reinforced with grenadiers and the pickets the points successively menaced by the enemy, who, repulsed in one spot, courageously began the assault of another, so that "every part of the entrenchments was successively attacked with the greatest vigour." Montcalm's *aides-de-camp* constantly brought him reports of the spirit and good humour of the soldiers in the battle. Referring to the delays of M. de Vaudreuil in the despatch of reinforcements, they were heard crying aloud:

> M. de Vaudreuil has sold the country, but f——, we will not permit him to deliver it. He has sacrificed us to make us cut the C——, let us defend them. Long live the King and our General.

Throughout the lines, the battalions showed no preoccupation save for one thing, to know if their flanks were safe. Whenever they heard an increase in the firing by the enemy, there was but one cry

Take care at the right, take care at the left.

The Engineer Desandrouins, sent on several occasions by Montcalm to the line of fire to report "whether they had need of support," everywhere received the same reply:

We have no need of support here, but take care lest there should be a need elsewhere.

With an admirable understanding of the human heart, Desandrouins shouted to the soldiers on the right and on the left, to each in turn, who asked for news of what was happening:

On the other wing, there are more than 1,500 English, with their bellies in the air; the others are routed and their column no longer dares to show itself. There remain only the wicked sharpshooters behind the stumps, whom they amuse themselves in dispersing. I had then the pleasure of witnessing the wildest transports of joy and of hearing them encouraging themselves to light by shouts of 'Long live the King!' On coming to another section, I made the same speech, appealing to the veterans by name and telling them: 'We will get them cheaply: you are all courageous and good marksmen. They no longer dare show themselves anywhere.'

Several times during the battle, torches made from wadding and cartridges, set fire to the abatis, but always amongst the soldiers were found volunteers to cross the parapet in the open and extinguish the flames in view of the enemy.

Certain incidents worthy of notice occurred during the battle. On the extreme left, some twenty barges and pontoons of the enemy debouched, almost at the beginning of the battle, from the mouth of Fall River, but the Duprat and de Bernard volunteers fired on them in passing, in conjunction with the grenadier company and the picket of Royal-Roussillon, under the orders of M. de Poulhariès, who had posted themselves on the banks of the river. The cannon of the fort, ably served by

M. de Louvicourt, lieutenant in the Royal Corps, who himself aimed the pieces, swamped two of the pontoons by a few shots. The remaining boats of the enemy retired and did not reappear during the day.

At the centre, the Berry battalion, under fire for the first time and largely composed of recruits, wavered for a moment. The soldiers even abandoned the parapet of the entrenchment; but before the companies of grenadiers had need to intervene, the officers gained control of their men and led them back "so promptly, the enemy did not perceive it."

At the centre also a misunderstanding of the two adversaries nearly allowed the English to enter our entrenchments. As the ensigns of the Guyenne regiment waved their flags every time they heard the cry "Long live the King!" the English believed it was a signal from their adversaries offering to surrender. They ran to the entrenchment uplifting their arms and crying: "Quarter, Quarter."

On our side, the soldiers, attributing the same intentions to the English, replied to them: "Lay down your arms, lay down your arms." The enemy not doing it and always advancing, a volley of musketry was fired by our men, who had half the body raised above the entrenchment, which, coming from all sides, few were able to escape.

On the extreme right, the Canadians and the marines were not attacked. M. de Lévis sent them two of the Queen officers: M. d'Hert, adjutant, and M. Desnoës, Captain, to get them to make a sortie and take the left column of the enemy on the flank, but without success, as only a few Canadians followed M. de Raymond and their officers. The greater part contented themselves with firing on the enemy at long range, although they had been reinforced, at about 4 o'clock, by 250 militia led by M. Duplessis, lieutenant, and Boisvert, clerk of commissary, who on landing at Carillon had come to increase the number of the defenders of the abatis on our right.

During four hours, the enemy renewed his attacks, which were "nearly everywhere of an equal violence." About 5 o'clock in the evening his two left columns were combined to make a supreme effort against the salient angle of the entrenchment defended by the right of Guyenne and the left of Béarn.

The space attacked by the doubled column did not exceed 20 fathoms; it was not fortified and dipped down; the enemy approached within half range tinder cover.

The Highlanders, who had not ceased to give proofs of the highest courage throughout the day, led the column to the assault. They reached the foot of the abatis and, for a moment, Montcalm feared the entrenchment would be entered at that point. He personally ran there with a party of Grenadiers and of the pickets, while the Chevalier de Lévis, seeing his right free of danger, doubled up, much to the purpose, the Queen battalion with those of Guyenne and Béarn. The assault broken by the fire of the defenders, the enemy were again obliged to retire, leaving the vicinity of the abatis covered with his dead. The Highlanders, of admirable courage, themselves alone, in killed and wounded had lost 25 officers and half of their effectives.

After this last supreme effort, the enemy attacks diminished in violence and, between 6 and 7 o'clock, they merely maintained a lire along the whole front by sharpshooters, so as to gain time to remove the wounded and cover the retreat of his columns to the camp of the Fall. Towards 7 o'clock, several soldiers of Béarn surmounted the entrenchment, put to flight or killed the sharpshooters, ambushed behind the nearest stumps of trees, and brought back some prisoners.

From them it was learned the English intended to renew the attack the next morning. These reports, the approach of night, "the exhaustion and the small number of our troops, the forces of the enemy, who though defeated, were still infinitely superior to ours, the character of the forest in which one may not enter without savages against an army which had 400 or 500, several entrenchments which the enemy had made, the one behind the other from the field of battle to the camp:" such were the obstacles which caused Montcalm to determine not to pursue the

English in their retreat.

One can readily believe, after the fatigues of these last two days our troops felt the need of some rest. During the battle each soldier had fired between 70 and 80 shots, which obliged them "to exchange a number of guns during the action," but cartridges were never lacking to the defenders. M. de Frecesson, commandant of the 3rd Berry battalion, had given his attention to supplying them with abundant ammunition, either with the assistance of carts, or with the help of men of his battalion who, without being on the firing line, did not escape some loss in the crossing from the fort to the entrenchments.

As the heat had been great during the entire day, Montcalm had also ordered that barrels of water should be conveyed from the fort to the entrenchments, a duty admirably performed by the 3rd Berry battalion.

Towards 7:30 o'clock, Montcalm ordered cease firing, it being sustained only by some marksmen ambushed on the borders of the forest. Then, accompanied by Chevalier de Lévis, he passed along the front of the battalions, happy to be able to thank and congratulate them on their extraordinary bravery. He was received with repeated acclamations.

After having taken some moments of repose, the troops passed the night cleaning their arms and in reinforcing the defence of the entrenchments, in anticipation of a renewed assault the next day. Lacking traverses, which they hastened to make, many sections of the lines had been subject to enfilade fire of the enemy, and, though our battalions fought under cover, they had suffered perceptible losses.

Amongst the Staff, M. de Bourlamaque had been seriously wounded in the shoulder, M. de Bougainville slightly in the head, Chevalier de Lévis had received two bullets through his hat.

The battalions lost 12 officers killed and 25 wounded, two of them mortally. The number of soldiers killed amounted to 92, that of the wounded to 248. The marines and the Canadians contributed to these losses 2 officers wounded, 10 soldiers killed

GENERAL THOMAS GAGE
With Abercrombie at Ticonderoga

and 11 wounded.

Though the French had lost in killed and wounded a tenth of their effectives, the English, more sorely tried, had to deplore the loss of 2,000 of theirs, about a sixth of the number of troops engaged. In his letter to Pitt, dated July 12, 1758, Abercrombie acknowledges "464 men of the regular troops killed, 29 missing, and 1,117 wounded; 87 men of the provincial militia killed, 8 missing and 239 wounded, the officers being included in the foregoing."

At dawn on the 9th July, our troops confidently awaited the renewal of the English assault, but opposite them nothing came to trouble the stillness of the forest. Companies of volunteers, sent out to reconnoitre, advanced even to the mill of the Fall without finding any further sign of the enemy than the remains of the boats which they had burned.

The 10th of July, Chevalier de Lévis, detached with the eight companies of grenadiers, the volunteers and about fifty Canadians, advanced as far as the Carry. He observed manifold signs of a precipitate flight on the part of the enemy.

Since early in the morning July 9th Abercrombie had retired to the north shore of Lake Saint Sacrement and his army, which three days ago had landed on this shore in admirable order, believing they were advancing to certain victory, so great was their confidence in their strength, re-embarked hastily, profoundly shaken in morale and, notwithstanding their superior numbers, quite incapable of facing the dangers of a renewed battle.

Fifteen thousand men fled from before three thousand. Canada was saved. The victory of our little army seemed such a prodigy, Montcalm and his soldiers ascribed it above all to divine intervention, to the "direct finger of Providence." Therefore, on the 12th July, the French general held a review of the battalions and had a *Te Deum* sung in grateful acknowledgment on the stage of the battle itself. The religious fervour of that army, the majestic frame of the scene, the grandeur of the forest now given up to silence and repose, the calm of the lakes and of the transparent waters of the rivers, with banks covered with luxuriant vegetation, all contributed to engrave ineffaceably on the minds of those present the memory of this day of triumph.

In all our military history there is probably no action wherein commander, officers and soldiers brought in higher relief the warlike qualities of our race. From the very beginning Montcalm clearly perceived the danger which menaced Carillon. He had only a handful of men to oppose to the English, a fort scarcely begun as a support and supplies for only a few days in store. Nevertheless he accepts the challenge, and, from the time of his arrival, far from taking refuge under the cannon of the fortress, he adopts a formation in echelon which would give the enemy an impression of a larger force and would permit him to delay the march of the enemy for some days, time sufficient to allow his soldiers, from whom he knew he could ask anything, to construct formidable entrenchments.

The choice of the position selected to defend Carillon and the order read to the troops on the eve of the battle, confer the highest honour on the appreciation of the situation and foresight of Montcalm. But he is shown to be a great commander especially in having realized, during the first manoeuvres of Abercrombie, that his adversaries hesitated and wavered, that a fatal blindness obsessed them and that they would fall before him as a prey. Besides, his coolness during those eight days never for a moment fails.

Thus, as he wrote to his mother, Montcalm had not "the least anxiety since June 30th," the day of his arrival at Carillon. He inspired with this calm confidence those near him, both officers and men, by whom he was adored and from whom he was certain of absolute support in the hour of danger. "Long live the King and our General!" was their rallying cry and under fire they lavished the bravery, the activity, the gaiety, which make of our soldiers a warlike tool of incomparable pliancy.

Modestly reserved after his victory, Montcalm thought only of attributing the glory of that day to his comrades in arms.

All the commanders of corps, (he writes to M. de Vaudreuil, the 9th of July), and in general, all the officers, behaved in

LORD VISCOUNT HOWE.

GEORGE AUGUSTUS, LORD HOWE
Killed at Ticonderoga, July 6, 1758

such a way that I can only claim the merit of finding myself the Commander of such valorous troops and fulfilling the duty of affording them support successively, as the sections of our abatis were more or less actively assaulted.

To his friend Doreil he made this magnificent tribute to the courage of our soldiers:

The Army, the very small army of the King, has vanquished its enemies. What a day for France! If I had had 200 savages to serve as guides to a detachment of 1,000 selected men, of which I would have entrusted the command to M. de Lévis, not many of them would have escaped in their flight. Ah! what troops, my dear Doreil, are these of ours! I have never seen any to equal them.

Then, as a sign revealing the deep affection of Montcalm for his valiant army, the day following the battle his only thought is given to obtain for them the most distinguished rewards of the King.

If there ever were a body of troops worthy of reward," he writes to Marshal de Belle-Isle the 12th of July, "it is the one I have the honour to command. So I beg of you, my lord, to surfeit them and grant them all that I have had the honour to propose to you.

For himself he only asks the favour to be recalled:

My health suffers, my purse is exhausted. I will be 10,000 écus in debt to the Treasurer General of the Colony at the end of the year and, more than anything else, the annoyances, the contradictions I experience, the impossibility as I am situated of doing good or preventing evil, determine me to earnestly beg His Majesty to grant this favour, my only ambition.

For his seconds, MM. de Lévis and de Bourlamaque, Montcalm declares he will only be satisfied if they are promoted to Major General and Brigadier:

If I have acquired any glory from this day, I share it with MM. de Lévis and de Bourlamaque and especially with the former, M. de Bourlamaque having had the misfortune to be wounded before the battle was over. I think, my lord, that far from any one being jealous of the promotion to Major General and Brigadier, which I entreat the King to grant them, one would rather feel astonished they had not obtained it.

The other officers of the staff were not forgotten. The rank of colonel is asked for M. de Bougainville, who "had been wounded" and possesses "talent and intelligence," also for Chevalier de Montreuil who "behaved on that day with much courage; of that I was confident, but also with an energy of which I did not think him capable. This officer should be at the head of a corps, he deserves favours. . . ." Montcalm emphasizes the valuable cooperation lent him at this decisive period for the safety of Canada by MM. de Pontleroy and Desandrouins:

> I cannot repeat too often, (he wrote to Marshal de Belle-Isle, the 29th of July, in a special memorandum), that the success (of the action on the 8th) was due to the abatis laid out and constructed by MM. de Pontleroy and Desandrouins; the former served the King excellently, in spite of the annoyances he encountered and for which vim should properly indemnify him. I shall be much obliged to you, if you treat him well; the latter, besides doing his duty, noted as my *aide-de-camp* on the day of the 8th. Therefore, I regard the Cross of St. Louis, which I solicit for him, as a personal favour.

In order to reward the leaders of corps, Montcalm asked for two Brigadierships: one for M. de Roquemaure, the ranking officer, who "conducted himself well" during the action of the 8th; the other for M. de Senezergues, who is only third in the order of seniority, after M. de Fontbonne;

> . . . . but M. de Senezergues, of our lieutenant colonels, is

MONUMENT TO LORD HOWE IN WESTMINSTER ABBEY

Inscription reads:—

The province of Massachusets Bay, in New England by an order of the great and general court bearing date Feby; 1st: 1759, caused this monument to be erected to the memory of George Augustus Lord Viscount Howe, Brigadier General of His Majesty's Forces in America, who was slain July the 6th 1758, on the march to Ticonderoga, in the 34th year of his age: in testimony of the sense they had of his services and military virtues, and of the affection their officers and soldiers bore to his command.

He lived respected and beloved: the publick regretted his loss; to his family it is irreparable.

the one most capable of commanding a corps with dignity, the one who is the busiest here and the only one you could trust at the peace, if two battalions were to be left for a year or two. He serves for honour and ambition, since he is of independent means. In the matter of creating two Brigadiers, of whom one is out of turn, I should feel inclined to favour him and augment the pension of M. de Fontbonne; if M. de Roquemaure alone is promoted, it should be evident from the reply to be made to me, the King knows there are other Lieutenant Colonels who might aspire to the same rank.

Besides, in a long memorandum Montcalm reviews the promotions and rewards due to particular officers. This work breathes the profound feeling of justice and equity which animated Montcalm and caused him to weigh, at their real value, the merits of each officer. Nothing, however, is comparable to the skill he exercised in making them conspicuous, without forgetting anyone.

When they learned at Versailles the details of this unexpected victory, which redounded so greatly to the honour of the French name, unqualified admiration arose for Montcalm and his brave army. Louis XV himself, shaking off his indifference, engaged the Bishops of the kingdom to chant a *Te Deum* in honour of the success carried off "by our brave soldiers in Canada." On his arrival at Court, Bougainville, despatched by Montcalm to present in its true light the critical situation of the Colony, heard the Marshal de Belle-Isle declare "in full audience, that if it were possible to create a *Maréchal de France* from a *Maréchal de Camp*, the King would have granted the favour to the Marquis de Montcalm."

Bougainville also had the pleasure of noting the whole of France associated itself in the wish of the King:

The entire Country has charged me with compliments for you, (he wrote to Montcalm, the 18th March 1759). . . . I should have to name all France if I tried to name all the persons who love you and hope to see you *Maréchal de France*. The little children know your name. . . .

During the month of March 1759 M. de Bougainville embarked at Bordeaux. He was entrusted with the memorandum containing the rewards from the King, proposed by Montcalm and recommended by Marshal de Belle-Isle, by which the eight French battalions in Canada were overwhelmed. Montcalm was raised to the rank of Lieutenant General, without further question of his recall, having himself renounced it. The capture of Louisburg, at the end of July 1758, and of Fort Frontenac, during the last days of August, made him foresee the early loss of Canada. heeling it was not the time to make recriminations, he forgot the humiliations and wounds to his self-respect and wrote to the Minister of War, the 9th of September 1758:

> I had asked for my recall after the glorious day of the 8th July, but, since the affairs of the Colony are going badly, it is for me to endeavour to repair them and delay the loss as much as I am able to do.

General, officers and soldiers learned through M. de Bougainville in the month of May 1759, that France, unable to send them any further reinforcements, abandoned them to their own resources, but this depressing news caused them no discouragement. The remembrance of their fatigues, of their dangers, of their isolation, vanished before the munificence of the royal rewards which diminished the importance of the most envied promotions.

No blame, no murmur was raised against the mother country and M. de Bougainville, a witness of the satisfaction of his comrades in arms, was able to write to the Minister of War, the 16th May 1759:

> The enormous force (of the English) is known, but that knowledge only serves to augment the zeal of the troops. The favours you have obtained for them, my lord, the assurance they have of the satisfaction of His Majesty, spread

Sir William Johnson, Baronet
In command of Indians
with Abercrombie

a joy and an enthusiasm, dissipating the hardships and dangers of all kinds which encompass us.

On learning of his promotion to Lieutenant General, Montcalm discreetly attributed the honour to the valour of his soldiers:

> Say to the troops, (he directed M. de Bourlamaque on the 15th of May 1759, then at Carillon), that I am very grateful for my promotion, which I owe to the distinguished manner in which they served under my orders.

To the Minister of War, the next day, he guaranteed that his little army and himself, by an unlimited devotion, would show their appreciation of the magnificent rewards of the King.

> ....I am as much overwhelmed as grateful for the favour His Majesty has granted in promoting me to the rank of Lieutenant General. This favour will add to my zeal for His service, if such a thing is possible. I am not less grateful for all that you have obtained for MM. de Lévis, de Bourlamaque, de Senezergues, de Montreuil, de Bougainville and to the corps of troops which I have the honour to command. We are probably on the eve of events which will make it possible to deserve more and more the kindness of His Majesty, and I dare promise you an absolute devotion to save this unhappy Colony or perish.

It is well known how Montcalm and his soldiers kept their word. A few months later, he himself fell like a hero, under the walls of Quebec.

Before abandoning a hopeless struggle, the victors of Carillon: The Queen, Béarn, Guyenne, Royal-Roussillon, Berry, Languedoc and La Sarre, unsupported save by their own courage, during a year still continued to dispute Canada with the invaders and astonished our enemies by the energy of their resistance.

Faithful to their past and to the memory of Montcalm, they shed a consoling ray of glory on those last days of New France, so dark and so imbued with sadness.

RIVER FROM LAKE GEORGE

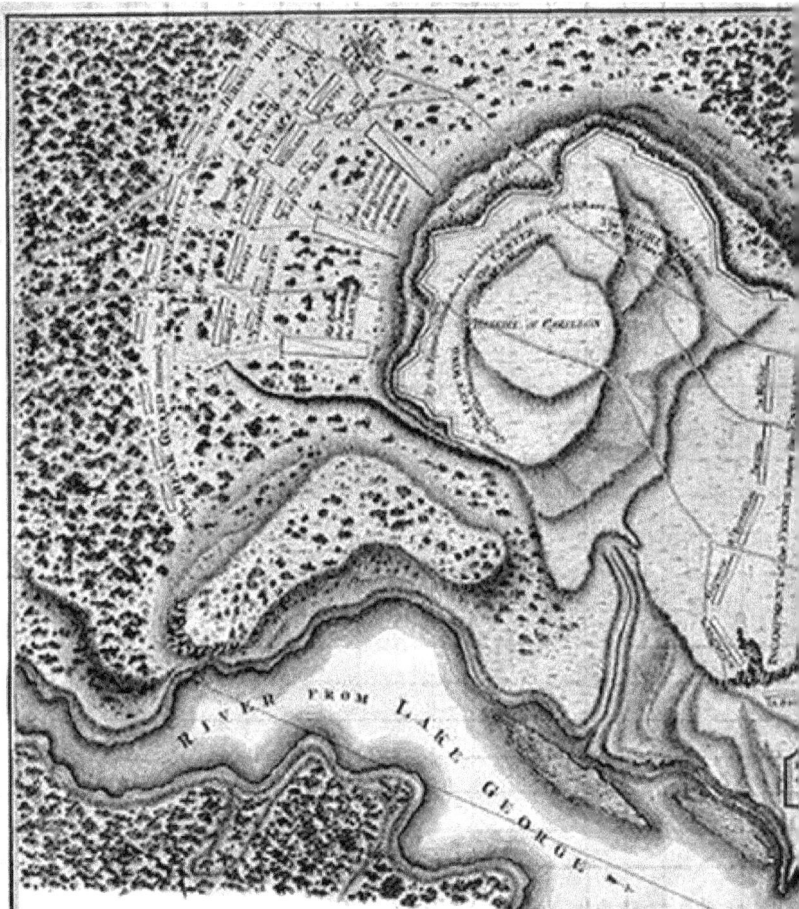

A PLAN of
the TOWN and FORT of
CARILLON
at
TICONDEROGA;
with
the ATTACK made by the
BRITISH ARMY
Commanded by Genl Abercrombie,
8 July 1758.
Engraved by
Thos Jefferys, Geographer to his Royal Highness the
PRINCE of WALES.

Scale of 250 Fathoms

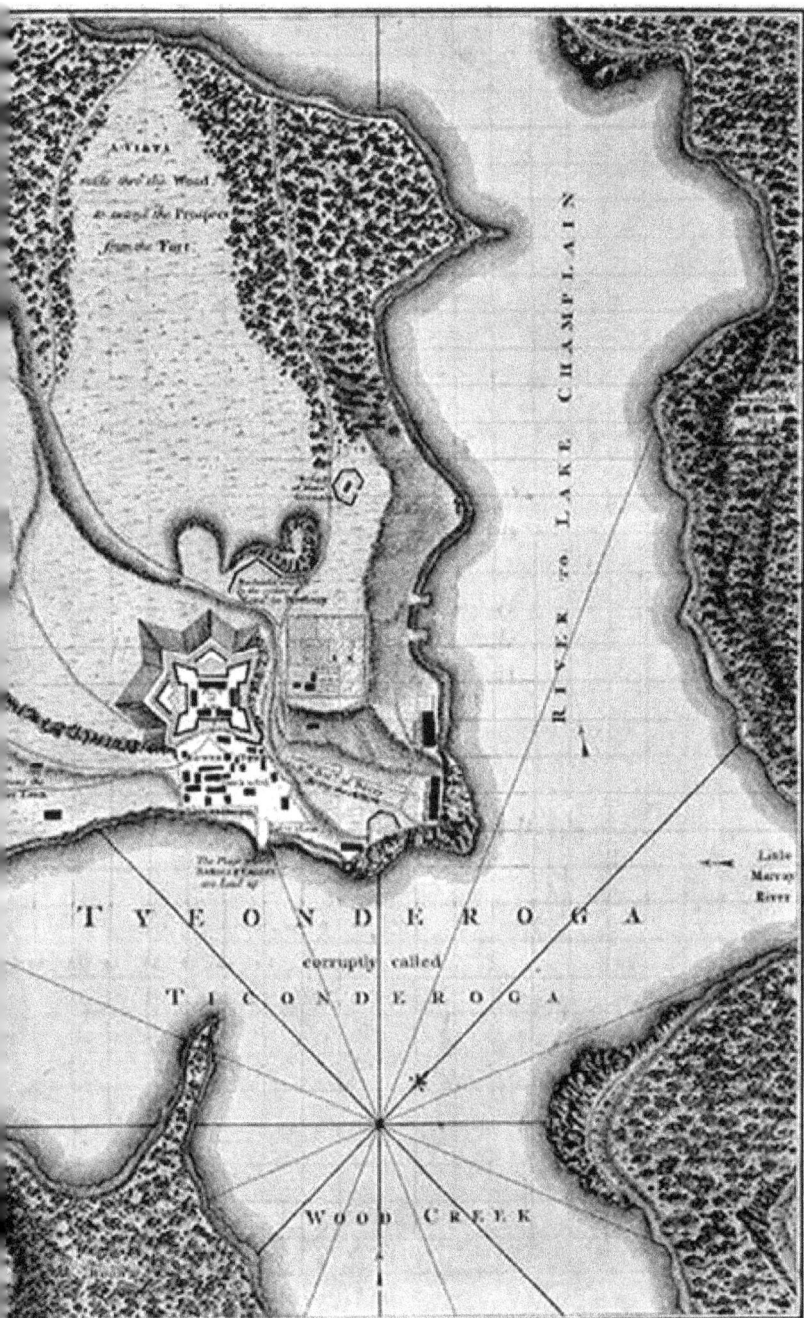

A VISTA
walk thro' the Wood
to augut the Prospect
from the Fort.

RIVER TO LAKE CHAMPLAIN

Little
Murray
River

T Y E O N D E R O G A

corruptly called

T I C O N D E R O G A

W O O D   C R E E K

LEONAUR

ALSO FROM LEONAUR
AVAILABLE IN SOFTCOVER OR HARDCOVER WITH DUST JACKET

FARAWAY CAMPAIGN *by F. James*—Experiences of an Indian Army Cavalry Officer in Persia & Russia During the Great War.

REVOLT IN THE DESERT *by T. E. Lawrence*—An account of the experiences of one remarkable British officer's war from his own perspective.

MACHINE-GUN SQUADRON *by A. M. G.*—The 20th Machine Gunners from British Yeomanry Regiments in the Middle East Campaign of the First World War.

A GUNNER'S CRUSADE *by Antony Bluett*—The Campaign in the Desert, Palestine & Syria as Experienced by the Honourable Artillery Company During the Great War .

DESPATCH RIDER *by W. H. L. Watson*—The Experiences of a British Army Motorcycle Despatch Rider During the Opening Battles of the Great War in Europe.

TIGERS ALONG THE TIGRIS *by E. J. Thompson*—The Leicestershire Regiment in Mesopotamia During the First World War.

HEARTS & DRAGONS *by Charles R. M. F. Crutwell*—The 4th Royal Berkshire Regiment in France and Italy During the Great War, 1914-1918.

INFANTRY BRIGADE: 1914 *by John Ward*—The Diary of a Commander of the 15th Infantry Brigade, 5th Division, British Army, During the Retreat from Mons.

DOING OUR 'BIT' *by Ian Hay*—Two Classic Accounts of the Men of Kitchener's 'New Army' During the Great War including *The First 100,000* & *All In It.*

AN EYE IN THE STORM *by Arthur Ruhl*—An American War Correspondent's Experiences of the First World War from the Western Front to Gallipoli-and Beyond.

STAND & FALL *by Joe Cassells*—With the Middlesex Regiment Against the Bolsheviks 1918-19.

RIFLEMAN MACGILL'S WAR *by Patrick MacGill*—A Soldier of the London Irish During the Great War in Europe including *The Amateur Army*, *The Red Horizon* & *The Great Push.*

WITH THE GUNS *by C. A. Rose & Hugh Dalton*—Two First Hand Accounts of British Gunners at War in Europe During World War 1- Three Years in France with the Guns and With the British Guns in Italy.

THE BUSH WAR DOCTOR *by Robert V. Dolbey*—The Experiences of a British Army Doctor During the East African Campaign of the First World War.

www.ingramcontent.com/pod-product-compliance
Lightning Source LLC
Chambersburg PA
CBHW031900090426
42741CB00005B/571